Low Down and Coming On

Low Down and Coming On

A FEAST OF DELICIOUS

AND DANGEROUS POEMS

ABOUT PIGS

Edited by James P. Lenfestey

Red Dragonfly Press
NORTHFIELD & RED WING
MINNESOTA
2010

Introduction, volume compilation, and notes are
  copyright © 2010 by James P. Lenfestey.
  All rights reserved. Printed in the United States of America.

ISBN 978-1-890193-22-5

Library of Congress Control Number: 2010935581

The material in this volume is reprinted with permission of the holders
  of copyright and publication rights. Acknowledgments for these
  permissions are included at the back of the book along with
  author information.

Designed and typeset by Scott King
  using ITC New Esprit® and Sava,
  digital typefaces designed by Jovica Veljovič

The text was printed in the United States of America
  on 30% recycled stock
  by Thomson-Shore, Inc., a worker owned company

The dustjacket was letterpress printed
  at the Red Dragonfly Press print shop
  at the Anderson Center in Red Wing, Minnesota

Published by Red Dragonfly Press
  307 Oxford Street
  Northfield, MN 55057

www.reddragonflypress.org

*All I hope to say in books, all that I ever hope to say,
is that I love the world.* E. B. WHITE

*The Bleat, the Bark, Bellows and Roar
Are Waves that Beat on Heaven's Shore.* WILLIAM BLAKE

*What does the pig think of the dawn?
They do not sing but hold it up
with their huge rosy bodies,
with their hard little hooves.* PABLO NERUDA

*O Isis my goddess,
my goddess Isis,
forget not thy pig.* DENISE LEVERTOV

Alas! The Pigs are an unhappy nation! PERCY BYSSHE SHELLEY

Only the pigs are holy... RODNEY JONES

Introduction

Homer is the first pig poet in the Western literary sty, his pig muse Circe. Circe turned Odysseus' pals into pigs, and we never forgave that. But perhaps they were lucky: they could grunt, root and be useful at death; in human form they died miserably at sea to feed nameless squid. The T'ang Dynasty (618-907) poet Cold Mountain took a practical Chinese whack at piggery, sensibly equating pigs (so far as we know first domesticated in Asia 10,000 years ago) and humans through our common ravenous and indiscriminate appetites. William Blake pioneered the Romantic revolution against the church and its machinations by casting his lot with the superior divinity of the pig, and, perhaps surprisingly, Robert Service in the 20th century did the same. Robert Southey in the 18th century penned a brutal English ode about snout-boring that is not all that great, but the copyright ran out so I'll include it. I love Carl Sandburg. You may remember fog's "little cat feet" but I remember "Chicago," "Hog Butcher for the World" with no apologies beginning and ending, "proud to be Hog Butcher...."

Many modern poets have stepped into the sty, some only once or twice, like Galway Kinnell and Philip Levine and Jim Moore (at my prompting), others more often, some with grace and quick feet and a good scratch behind the ears and a successful dive in the pond slime, others slipping and sliding in stench and running for their lives when Her Hogness gives that determined look.

David Lee is unquestionably the greatest pig poet of modern times (his Canadian pig-tail cousin John B. Lee and Denise Levertov runners-up). His hog devotion includes raising them, chasing them, being bitten by them, eating them, and writing poems about them in not one but two sublime collections, *The Porcine Legacy* and *The Porcine Canticles*, and he's not entirely able to stay away from them in other collections either. To add to our amazement, his pork poems earned him the first Poet Laureateship of Utah, so literary triumph was involved, though pig poets generally shouldn't count on it. Still, pig poetry is not necessarily just for fun and bacon — humility, sanity and publication can be reasonable expectations, at least in the case of this corpulent anthology.

Here you will find a modern feast from the sublime to the delicious, behaviors from sweet to possessed, and companionship from the green ooze of our youth to the savage inutility of muddy old age. Here you will find portraits of pigs mean and happy and vengeful and lazy and fat and meager and fanciful, most (but not all) of them ending the same – with a climb up the ramp, not a turn out to pasture. You'll be here for the beginning and the end, the squeal and the scream.

On our piggish human plates, we pile hocks and jowls and hams and knuckles and ribs and loins and chops and bacon and sausage and wurst which is German for sausage and sucklings which are apple-sweet babies. But pigs are food not only for our bodies but for our poets. Perhaps it is the beautiful long eyelashes over mysterious eyes, or the gargantuan appetites, or the hairy feral tuskers hiding under the veneer of pink domesticity, or the similarity of our organs and anxieties, that has attracted so many poets. Or just the fun and hunger of it.

I have been hungry for this collection for three decades, ever since poet, essayist and raconteur Bill Holm first suggested it in print. With his blessing, issued before he shocked us with his untimely death in 2009, I am pleased to serve up this platter of pig poems to readers with all the trimmings, including the sizzle. Not the TAO of pigs, but the COLD MOUNTAIN of Pigs. These are poems you can EAT!

James P. Lenfestey
Minneapolis, spring, 2010

A note on proper pig diction. Most good English and American pig poetry instinctively tastes of robust earthy Anglo-Saxon, as the animal has rooted in English livestock yards and consciousness well before the arrival of the Latinate "pork," "the other white meat" for more elegant tables. The language of these poems represents a feast of Old English, Germanic and Gaelic root words of piggishness – hog, sow, sty, boar, shoat, gilt, farrow, stifle, suckling, swine, trotters and "root" itself, a verb meaning what pigs do to pastures or woodlots or backyards if given half a chance, that is to say turn over great swaths of sod with their powerful snouts (Middle English) to feed on spidery roots and fat grubs and fragrant truffles and ancient bones. The word "pig" itself is rooted in the Old English *picbred* meaning, literally, acorn, i.e. pig food.

In addition, English usage codified since the 15th Century makes sharp distinctions between collections of creatures versus individuals, as described in the timelessly delightful volume by James Lipton, *An Exaltation of Larks*. We hunt a *singular* of boars, raise a *sounder* of swine, follow a *drift* of hogs. The less poetic Wikipedia turns up an additional *drove* of pigs, *fleet* of pigs, *mob* of pigs and the now common *herd* of pigs, plus a *farrow* of piglets and the lovely *waltz* of piglets. The word *anthology*, from ancient Greek, means literally a gathering of flowers. What should English speakers term a gathering of pig poems? A serving? A platter? A feast?

A note on proper pig relations. Something awful happened on the way to the second half of the 20th century. Factory farming took a ghastly turn, confining pigs to body-sized enclosures throughout their entire lifetimes for the purpose of producing uniform hams. In such a situation pigs, like humans, go mad, meat softened by attacks of their own stress hormones. Not to mention the problem with massive lagoons of pig waste, nauseating downwind and sometimes downstream.

Pigs and humans have been buried together as friends for 10,000 years, a generous symbiosis. We have killed and eaten them by the billions, they have killed and eaten more than a few of us, but for the most part have been happy to fatten on the scraps of our tables, the acorns of our woods, the grubs of our fields. But they are happy pigs no longer under these madhouse conditions, a situation presciently anticipated by Shelley 190 years ago: *Alas! The Pigs are an unhappy nation!*

Alternatives exist. A couple decades ago cooks at small, often organic restaurants – in Philadelphia, Minneapolis, California – wanted to serve pork, but only if humanely pasture-raised, and so they taught farmers again how to do so. Now "pasture-raised" pig is available almost everywhere.

We praise with this book the steady return toward happy pigs "with one bad day," and challenge consumers of pig poetry to insist that "pasture-raised" become a necessary pre-condition to the sweetness of summer barbeque, the warmth of winter loins, the necessity of holiday hams and breakfast bacon, and yes, even the mystical contemplation of hot dogs roasted over campfires in the company of innocent human children.

As you will read below, we humans love our pigs, and should not tolerate the corruption of their flesh and minds. To paraphrase William Blake: *The Snuffle, Snort, Oink and Squeal/ reveal the state of the Commonweal.*

For Bill Holm,
born in 1943 on a pig farm in Swede Hollow, Minnesota,
interred in 2009 in nearby in Minneota, Minnesota,
in between loved life piggishly, and wrote like an angel, were an angel huge
and red-bearded and Scotch-drinking and humane and funny and wise,
and whose idea this anthology was.

Special gratitude to Robert Hedin, poet and anthologist extraordinaire, for
suggesting many early poems for this anthology.

And to Thomas R. Smith,
poet who not only "gets" pigs but pig anthologies.

And for
Blue Spot,
Yorkshire sow.

Contents

7	Introduction		**Sharon Chmielarz**
17	Prologue: The Secret Pig	39	Left to Herself, a Pig Will Be a Pig
	Anonymous	40	The Pig Next Door to Beethoven
19	The Lady That Loved a Swine		**Naomi Cohn**
	Anonymous	41	After a Lifetime Nose to Tail with Other Pigs
20	The Sow Took the Measles		**Billy Collins**
	Margaret Atwood	43	This Little Piggy Went to Market
21	Pig Song		**Melanny Cowley**
	Coleman Barks	44	Death on the Ranch
22	Pigs' Ears		**Josephine Dickinson**
23	The Hog Poet	46	Some Pig
	Tree Bernstein		**Russell Edson**
24	Regarding Pigs	47	A Performance at Hog Theater
	Wendell Berry		**Heid E. Erdrich**
26	For the Hog Killing	48	Long Pig
	William Blake		**Louise Erdrich**
27	I Saw a Chapel	49	Pig
	Carol Bly		**Martín Espada**
28	Slopping the Hogs on the Vonderharr's Farm	50	Cade Puerco Tiene Su Sábado
		52	DSS Dream
	Robert Bly		**Jane Gentry**
29	The Prodigal Son	53	Portrait of the Artist as a White Pig
30	Iseult and the Badger		**Jane Graham George**
31	Rembrandt's Etchings	54	Swine Judging, Dakota County Fair
	Dan Bohnhorst		**Donald Hall**
32	Solstice Fire	55	Eating the Pig
	Todd Boss		**Susan Thurston Hamerski**
33	Yellowrocket	59	Sows I Have Known
	Jill Breckenridge		**Han-shan**
37	Pretty Ricky	60	"Pigs devour..."
	Michael Dennis Browne		**Margaret Hasse**
38	State Fair Song	61	Beauty Parading Main Street

John Southall Hatcher
62 Pig Thoughts at Noon
64 Pig Song
67 The Mighty Anglo-Saxon
    Hog Uprising

Robert Hedin
69 Sainte-Foy
70 Tornado

Tom Hennen
71 Sunlight After the Pig Yard Flood

William Heyen
72 Pig Notes

Jim Heynen
74 Tornado Alert
77 During Spring Floods
78 Farrowing Pen
80 Sometimes a Sow

Bill Holm
82 Pig
83 Old Sow on the Road

Ted Hughes
84 The Pig

Colette Inez
86 Little Pig of Beauty

John Janovy, Jr.
87 God Loved Pigs

Louis Jenkins
88 Leoti

Rodney Jones
89 The Eating of Swine

Scott King
91 *Demons*

Susan Deborah King
93 Ambivalence

Galway Kinnell
95 St. Francis and the Sow
96 The Sow Piglet's Escape

William Kloefkorn
97 Two poems from *Alvin Turner*
    As Farmer
99 Ludi, jr. as the Hired Hand Pays
    Dearly for What He is Paid For

Ted Kooser
102 Wild Pigs

Kathryn Kysar
103 When Pigs Fly: Kurt's Diary

Julie Landsman
104 Property Values

Kristin Laurel
105 Rescue

David Lee
107 Loading a Boar
108 Culture
109 Epilogue

John B. Lee
112 Shouting Who We Are
114 Pig Dentistry
116 Pretend You Are Happy

Jay Leeming
117 Pig Teachings

Gabrielle Lemay
118 Turpentine

James P. Lenfestey
120 Roadkill Bacon
121 What the Smell of Frying Bacon
     Means to Me
123 What the Smell of Frying Bacon
     Means to Him
124 Sow Haiku

Nathaniel "Max" Lenfestey
125 A Man Who Loves His Bacon

Denise Levertov
126 Her Judgment
128 Her Vision
129 Her Prayer

Philip Levine
130 Animals Are Passing from Our Lives

Perie Longo
131 Between Piglet and Pug

Frederick Manfred
132 from *Green Earth*

Elizabeth McKim
133 When the Elevator Stopped We Just Had to Look Around

Tom Meyer
135 Eating Chrome

Charles H. Miller
137 Confessions of a Rebel Robot

David E. Moody
140 The Last Days of Suza's Pet Pig

Jim Moore
142 Blood in Our Headlights, the Car Wrecked, the Boar Dead

Pablo Neruda
143 Bestiary

Margaret Noori / Giiwedinoodin
148 Words of Wiiyaas

Don Olsen
149 Pigs

Joe Paddock
150 Henry and Hilda
153 Hog Hunger

Greg Pape
156 The Hog Boss

Linda Pastan
158 Gleaning

Sylvia Plath
159 Sow

Jeff Poniewaz
161 Rush Hour Freeway Spill

Vasko Popa
163 Pig

John Calvin Rezmerski
164 Missionary Work

George Roberts
165 Pig

Pattiann Rogers
166 Boar: Even Though
168 Selene's Generosity

Edith Rylander
170 Old Man Stuckel Talks to the Hogs

Jay Salter
172 Emergence
173 Moonlight
174 *Sus Scrofa*, or Wild Boar

Carl Sandburg
175 Chicago

Robert W. Service
176 The Junior God

Anne Sexton
177 Hutch

Martin Shaw
178 The Briny Tusk

Percy Bysshe Shelley
180 Oedipus Tyrannus, or, Swellfoot the Tyrant

Jason Shinder
181 Pigs

Robert Siegel
184 The White Sow of Marengo

Patricia Smith
185 What Keeps Playing on the B Side

Thomas R. Smith
186 Pigskin

Gary Snyder
187 Sus

Robert Southey
188 Ode

Anne Running Sovik
190 Pig Beauty

Barry Spacks
191 Singing the Pig

David Steingass
192 Riding the Moon-Pig

Joseph Stroud
193 from 'I Wanted to Paint Paradise'

Su Dongpo
194 On the Birth of His Son
195 Dongpo Pork

Joyce Sutphen
197 What's Time to a Pig?

David Wagoner
198 The Orchard of the Dreaming Pigs

Robert Penn Warren
199 Go It Granny — Go It, Hog!

Cary Waterman
200 After the Pig Butchering
202 Pig Poem

Jackson Wheeler
203 Hog Killing Memory

Jay P. White
204 On Any Given Day

Walt Whitman
206 That's No Metaphor on the Streets of Brooklyn

Morgan Grayce Willow
207 Farrow

Kevin Young
210 Ode to Pork
211 Ode to Chitlins

Timothy Young
214 A Black Pig's Head
215 A Son of the Boar of Dartmoor

Brad Zellar
216 Pig Tents

Patricia Zontelli
217 With Love, *Piggy*

Permissions & Author Bios

James P. Lenfestey

PROLOGUE: THE SECRET PIG
*— After hearing pig poems read aloud, she came up to me
with this poetic tale*

The Secret Pig
came to her in a dream
accompanied by filthy boys
dressed in rags.
"May we keep our Secret Pig
at your house?" they inquired.
"Yes, yes, if you must," she answered.
"In the garage... the back yard.
If I need help, I'll call
my nephew. He's a poet.
He knows all about these secret pigs."

Anonymous

THE LADY THAT LOVED A SWINE

There was a lady loved a swine,
 "Honey!" quoth she;
"Pig-hog, wilt thou be mine?"
"Hoogh!" quoth he.

"I'll build thee a silver sty,
 Honey!" quoth she;
"And in it thou shalt lie!"
"Hoogh!" quoth he.

"Pinned with a silver pin,
 Honey!" quoth she;
"That thou mayest go out and in,"
"Hoogh!" quoth he.

"Wilt thou have me now,
 Honey?" quoth she;
"Speak or my heart will break,"
"Hoogh!" quoth he.

Recited by James Wright
New York City, March 2, 1967

Anonymous

THE SOW TOOK THE MEASLES

How do you think I begin in the world?
I got me a sow and sev'ral other things.
The sow took the measles, and she died in the spring.

What do you think I made of her hide?
The very best saddle that you ever did ride.
Saddle or bridle or any such thing,
The sow took the measles, and she died in the spring.

What do you think I made of her nose?
The very best thimble that ever sewed clothes.
Thimble or thread or any such thing,
The sow took the measles and she died in the spring.

What do you think I made of her tail?
The very best whup that ever sought sail
Whup or whup-socket, any such thing,
The sow took the measles, and she died in the spring.

What do you think I made of her feet?
The very best pickles that you ever did eat.
Pickles or glue or any such thing,
The sow took the measles, and she died in the spring.

19th century American folksong collected by Katharine Grant

Margaret Atwood

PIG SONG

This is what you changed me to:
a grey pink vegetable with slug
eyes, buttock
incarnate, spreading like a slow turnip,

skin you scuff so you may feed
in your turn, a stinking wart
of flesh, a large tuber
of blood which munches
and bloats. Very well then. Meanwhile

I have the sky, which is only half
caged, I have my weed corners,
I keep myself busy, singing
my song of roots and noses,

my song of dung. Madame,
this song offends you, these grunts
which you find oppressively sexual,
mistaking simple greed for lust.

I am yours. If you feed me garbage,
I will sing a song of garbage.
This is a hymn.

PIGS' EARS

One Saturday night
to make an event
I bought pigs' ears
at the Colonial store.
It would be something
to talk about I knew
as I asked the Negro woman
at the meat counter what
I should do with them.
Boil them for an hour.
Which made the leathery
cartilage pink and soft
as any young thing's ear
on my cannibal plate like
a last-minute blind date
(and deaf).
          I really had
rather eat a silk purse.

Coleman Barks

THE HOG POET

Everybody lie back
& have a snort.

Spread the goodies out
where the sun can hit

porkchop, fatback
hackles & hooves.

Asspay the aconbay
Asspay the knife.

Food is the before.
Song the afterlife.

༄

Compadres, ah
cement compadres,

this is not all
there is — trough,

pool & nap. Gruffle
through your nose

that gods will wake
& feed their children

counting piggies
in their toes.

Tree Bernstein

REGARDING PIGS
— *For Hayden Carruth 1921-2008*

The first time the pigs went to farrow, my Daddy
stayed the night in the shed with them, making sure the sows
were all right & none of the piglets got stepped on.
After he hurt his back roofing & the sugar beets didn't
bring in as expected, he lost interest, I guess.
Next season the sows were left to drop
their litters in the muck alone.

Daddy said I could have my pick for 4-H.
I unwisely chose a black-faced Berkshire that I called Charlotte.
She was a runt to begin with, never even topped 60 pounds
when it came time to sell her at auction.
She was no blue-ribbon pig, but cute, as far as pigs go.
Charlotte came when I called.
When Daddy brought in the neighbor's old sire to mount her,
I thought she'd smother under his weight.
She farrowed in the chute, rolled over on two of her babies,
so we only got four out of that litter.

We had bantams who picked their way daintily
through the mud pen & ate expelled grain
& phantom bugs no one else could see.
The rooster, who was more cock than doodle-doo,
never noticed the rat stealing his hen's eggs.
Daddy found the rat's nest in the corner of the shed
under a milk crate; the old fella apparently ate in bed —
there were egg shells & other scraps, a couple of bottle caps,
my lost silver-colored barrette & one shiny dime.
He also had two dead half-hatched chicks,
bald-headed with eyes X-ed out.
Daddy had me hold the garden hose over the rat's hole.
We'd flush him out.
The ground heaved & rumbled. The rat's pointed nose,
then yellow teeth broke through the earth.

Daddy stuck a pitchfork clean through his neck.
The pigs watched from their side of the pen.

Mr. Smith took the 5th grade class over to
the slaughterhouse in Moses Lake for Enrichment.
We were all glad to go, packed with our
bologna sandwiches on the dusty yellow school bus.
He'd already taken us to the County Jail & Carnegie Library.
We were all farm kids, we knew where meat came from.
We just didn't know how it was taken.
The pigs marched single-file up to the man
with a black rubber apron,
who slit their throats, one after another.
On the farm, pigs squealed.
At the slaughterhouse, they screamed.
They screamed on after their bellies opened
& dropped grey entrails onto the cement floor.
Then they were silent.

So were we
on the bus
all the way home,
where our mothers waited supper for us —
green beans, mashed potatoes & pork chops.

Wendell Berry

FOR THE HOG KILLING

Let them stand still for the bullet, and stare the shooter in the eye,
let them die while the sound of the shot is in the air, let them die as
      they fall,
let the jugular blood spring hot to the knife, let its freshet be full,
let this day begin again the change of hogs into people, not the
      other way around,
for today we celebrate again our lives' wedding with the world,
for by our hunger, by this provisioning, we renew the bond.

William Blake

I SAW A CHAPEL

I saw a chapel all of gold
That none did dare to enter in,
And many weeping stood without,
Weeping, mourning, worshipping.

I saw a serpent rise between
The white pillars of the door,
And he forc'd and forc'd and forc'd,
Down the golden hinges tore.

And along the pavement sweet,
Set with pearls and rubies bright,
All his slimy length he drew
Till upon the altar white

Vomiting his poison out
On the bread and on the wine.
So I turn'd into a sty
And laid me down among the swine.

Carol Bly

SLOPPING THE HOGS ON THE VONDERHARR'S FARM
— For Emil and the memory of Marge Vonderharr

I go over to slop the hogs at the Vonderharr's farm,
And they come running up —
Candy? Their eyes say.
Cigarettes? Their eyes say.
Women? Their eyes say.
And their eyes say,
Peace on earth, good will toward men.

Robert Bly

THE PRODIGAL SON

The Prodigal Son is kneeling in the husks.
My friend, the steering column in his chest,
Cried: "Don't let me die, Doctor!"
The swine go on feeding in the sunlight.

When he folds his hands, his knees
On corncobs, he sees the smoke of ships
Floating off the isles of Tyre and Sidon,
And father beyond father beyond father.

An old man once, being dragged across
The floor by his shouting son, cried:
"Don't drag me any farther than that crack on the floor —
I only dragged my father that far!"

So this dragging of father and son goes on
Century after century after century.
There are brothers, some favorites, some
Not. Neither brother gets what he wants.

My father is seventy-five years old.
Looking at his face, I look into water.
How difficult it is! Under the water
There's a door that the pigs have gone through.

Robert Bly

ISEULT AND THE BADGER

The ink we write with seeps in through our fingers.
What we call reason is the way the parasite
Learns to live in the saint's intestinal tract.

Even the finest reason still contains the darkness
From feathers packed together; General Patton
Was a salmon who grew large in the Etruscan pool.

All our language is woven from animal hair.
The badgers and the thrushes soak up the stain of separation,
Just as lanolin makes the shearer's hands soft.

The old thinkers of quiddity remind us
Of the fear the hogs feel hanging by their hind legs;
For we know our throats are open to the unfaithful.

"I was climbing on the sounds of my lover's
Name toward God," Iseult said. "Then a badger ran past.
When I said, 'Oh badger,' I fell to earth."

Perhaps if we used no words at all in poems
We could continue to climb, but things seep in.
We are porous to the piled leaves on the ground.

Robert Bly

REMBRANDT'S ETCHINGS

The cross-hatching brings the night into the day,
Just as the donkey brings its cargo into Egypt.
I am a beggar reaching out my hand for darkness.

The cat can't explain how much the mouse loves
Its teaspoon of darkness; nor we why we sip
So thirstily from the pond made with a sharp stylus.

What is this? A monk and a girl in the corn?
He can no more keep his seed from rising
Than the kernel prevent the corn from coming up.

The resting hog is content, tied by one leg,
At least for now. She is far down on the earth;
And no longer remembers small boys or boiling water.

Joseph needs a lantern as he and Mary
Travel silently through the night. The donkey
Is about to put its hoof down in that darkness.

The hatching and shadowiness are everywhere.
The lion, standing by the pollarded willow,
Protects the old St. Jerome while he reads.

Dan Bohnhorst

SOLSTICE FIRE

We are nursed by the fire.
Milk flows from the flames.

Like suckling pigs,
Our veins will soon run dry

But for now we feast
On the light.

The lamps of our eyes
Glow through the smoke.

O my squinting piglets,
Remember this heat

In your beds tonight,
Hold in your hearts

This flickering beast
Burning on her side,

Giving her hot milk
Freely and without end.

YELLOWROCKET

Filthy, but still of good
tilth, our new bargain 80
(40 high, 40 hinter)
made us instantly
wealthy with rubbish.

Never buy a farm
in winter. For years,
my mother stood
by my father's side
in thickets choked

with tractor parts
and bedcoil and
cried. Whether grief
or shame or the fact
that people could be

such pigs more
upset her, I never
knew. Didn't matter.
Whatever it was
filled up our

quarter-ton Ford a
hundred times over.
The work was clay
deep, the debt was
north slope steep.

We could've driven
State Highway 27
to the local dump in
our sleep. I grew up in
boiled wool jackets,

thinking soil smelled
like brushfire smoke.
Had holes been coins,
our gloves and boots
would've jangled.

Unwitting heirs, we'd
come into a garden
overgrown with plastic
diapers and broken
furniture tangled in

burdock and brambles
and thistle. We'd split
with family and moved
a hundred miles, and
the gamble's payout

was piles of bent nails
and moldering shingle.
Some messes called
for rake, others shovel.
Either way, by dusk of

day we were down
on our knees picking
window glass shards
from the muck. If we
rested, we rested from

wresting long twists
of rusted barbed wire
from deepening kinks
of birches. Primal
was our desire to take

that junk-pile back
from the skunk and
the snake and the rat.
We were the unsung
angels of our portion

of the plat. And for
all that, on Sundays
the Lord gave us halos
of hat-hair and gnats,
and then, in due season:

the apple's blossom,
forest floors dappled
with trillium, fields
of tall corn, a barn not
yet fallen, views of the

countryside patterned
with drifting pollen,
berries by the bucketful,
the otherworldly lull
of the breeze in our

break of white pines,
5-wire fences posted
in good straight lines,
the easy spirals
of the golden eagles

that nested in our
hardwoods' crowns,
the kind of sky
in which a small boy
drowns, our health,

and a feel for the earth
indistinct from
scorn. Call it love,
but if you call it love,
call it a love that

persisted, that
stained the palms
and reeked when
you pulled it,
like yellowrocket.

Jill Breckenridge

PRETTY RICKY

He's 1200 pounds of pink pork covered by black
bristles stiff enough to needle and sew with,
Pretty Ricky, all six feet of him spread
out, asleep, no fancy dancer, neither twirler
nor prancer, just eats and sleeps, the biggest
boar at the Fair, oblivious to gawkers, smirkers,
cholesterol, or weight watchers, fat off the hoof,
fat lying flat, good only for breeding and eating,
he won't even stand to show off all the pork cuts
displayed on the poster behind him: ham, it says,
oldest meat of civilized man, from the butt;
kabobs from the shoulder, roasted on swords
by early Asian nomads; spareribs, sausage,
and bacon from the belly. Pretty Ricky urges
me to swear off pork, but it's lunchtime and my
stomach wanders off to a foot-long or a brat with
'kraut. I think twice, three times, waffle back
and forth between meat and a veggie wrap, as, in
front of me, many meals stretch out, dozing.

Michael Dennis Browne

STATE FAIR SONG

I want to learn to sleep
like the pigs at the State Fair;
oh, how those swine could sleep!
Teach me! Teach me!

Like princes
in palaces
of straw

        Snore...   Snore...

there they lay,

Like hairy
like milky
kings
slumped on their thrones

        Snore...   Snore...

there they lay.

How do you do it, hogs?
The secret, the secret!
Snort me your secret
from the barns of sleep,
O swine!
Teach me! Teach me!

      Snore...
               Snore...
                        Snore...

Sharon Chmielarz

LEFT TO HERSELF, A PIG WILL BE A PIG

She saw most clearly with her snout.
She wandered under the Tree's green
cloud of miniature red moons and
hoggily snuffled the fragrant windfall.
God heard her snorting, her grunting
gorging on the delicious; that swish
in her waddle caught His great ear,
before He wept over the handfuls of air
where His apples used to be. He called
her a pig, a hog, a get-out-of-here.
On the run she devised a muddy Hereafter
with a wavering scent of the divine.

Sharon Chmielarz

THE PIG NEXT DOOR
TO BEETHOVEN

Who's heard of Beethoven's neighbor's hog,
Siegfried, who hungered after romance,
that is, to be transported from his pen,
and was every time Beethoven's window
stood open? Heart throbbing, ears
flapping wider as a crescendo rose,
Siegfried wallowed at a trill's tenderness,
a cadenza's cascade, rushing like a stream
in spring to complete itself. His eyes
paled at a sostenuto's shimmer. On stuffy days,
a concerto in G seemed the only breathless
hope that kept him from going feral.

Naomi Cohn

AFTER A LIFETIME NOSE TO TAIL WITH OTHER PIGS

the only newness in the truck
is the world rumbling beneath you
and a sense that, beyond the familiar smell of pig,
is something else, mechanical, gassy and cold
and then

the truck overturns and
you are free —

cars blaring past
frozen blacktop under your trotters
chorus of squealing hogs
still trapped in the truck.

Terrifying, the cold on the skin,
disorienting, that tumble
before scrambling out
into Minnesota December,
19 degrees, pale sun just rising.

Dawn's cloudy, but more light
than you've ever seen,
glimpsed as you toss
the great notched flaps of your ears.
It makes you blink.

The metal staple bitten into your ear,
holding the numbered tag —
08 dash 4673 —
burns with coldness.

The shit smell that has been your whole life
vanishes,
swept away by the wind and diesel.

You don't know what snow is,
but each flake pricks
as it melts on your pink back.

The earth's hardness is shocking
not the usual slippery dung and dropped corn kernels.

Running is so new —
mass wobbling as you slow-motion scamper
into the swale that divides
the rattling streams of cars and trucks,
ferocious light eyes staring red and white

 so strange

and then more cars with sirens and lights.
They stop and pour out men swearing.
You've heard this before.
They shout and wave their arms
so you gallop, show surprising speed

and soon
you are lonely, hungry, winded and cold
but you keep dodging the yelling
because this must be heaven
and you want to stay
as long as you can.

Billy Collins

THIS LITTLE PIGGY WENT TO MARKET

is the usual thing to say when you begin
pulling on the toes of a small child,
and I have never had a problem with that.
I could easily picture the piggy with his basket
and his trotters kicking up the dust on an imaginary road.

What always stopped me in my tracks was
the middle toe — this little piggy ate roast beef.
I mean I enjoy a roast beef sandwich
with lettuce and tomato and a dollop of horseradish,
but I cannot see a pig ordering that in a delicatessen.

I am probably being too literal-minded here —
I am even wondering why it's called "horseradish."
I should just go along with the beautiful nonsense
of the nursery, float downstream on its waters.
After all, Little Jack Horner speaks to me deeply.

I don't want to be the one to ruin the children's party
by asking unnecessary questions about Puss in Boots
or, again, the implications of a pig eating beef.
By the way, I am completely down with going
"Wee wee wee" all the way home,
having done that many times and knowing exactly how it feels.

Melanny Cowley

DEATH ON THE RANCH

Beneath the Russian Olive,
I kill the sparrow
several hundred yards away
with a pellet gun
when I am twelve.
I didn't think I would hit it,
a brown body warm in sand,
tiny feathers spread in a wave.

At fourteen, I wound a rabbit
that needs to be finished.
Dad beside me in the desert brush,
we walk closer for a better shot.
Its eyes black circles
hunched in shaking gray fluff,
I hand over the gun and he fires.

My uncle's geese
squawk impatience,
peck at us greedily,
shit on the steps,
I didn't feel bad
when Paul wrung their necks.

But every fall, there's the pigs.
Sageful eyes,
they grunt gratitude
at rotted watermelon.
I pet their scratchy heads.

One fall, the aim is wrong.
My kids cannot see
but still, I carry them
from the squeals floating over us.
The men say it was a bad death.

My father, my husband, and I
spend two days skinning,
scraping and sawing,
grinding sausage through a grater,
wrapping ribs in white paper.

Paul throws some sausage on the grill,
and for a moment we cease, exhausted.
He hands me the meat and says,
Isn't it good?

And it is good,
but there's a knot in my gut,
knowing the sweet, placid creatures,
not at all like the geese,
who were delicious.

With the tub of wrapped pig
in my arms
I step through the bite of late fall,
place the heavy meat
on the rusting blue tailgate
of the eighty-six Ford.

A sparrow
perches on a Russian Olive,
peers at me,
hops,
and flies north.

Josephine Dickinson

SOME PIG

Although I could think of a few things to say about the pig they would not be grounded in experience of a living pig.

However, it is true to say that the china pig stood behind the framed picture of an apple listing several varieties for sale, and that, as if to snuffle up the precious fruit,

His snout was down, and he displayed the black down on his floppy ears, pointing presumably at the five pips that he would presently reveal

And in just moments from now grind in his as yet invisible gnashers and that his black trotters were planted firmly as he nosed avant.

He looked like a contented pig – no doubt because he was conceptual,

And so he existed in the same world as and took his nourishment from ideas,

And so he would be a good pig to write a poem about,

Notwithstanding he'd rather be the boss of a Michelin three-starred restaurant.

Russell Edson

A PERFORMANCE AT HOG THEATER

There was once a hog theater where hogs performed as men, had men been hogs.

One hog said, I will be a hog in a field which has found a mouse which is being eaten by the same hog which is in the field and which has found the mouse, which I am performing as my contribution to the performer's art.

Oh let's just be hogs, cried an old hog.

And so the hogs streamed out of the theater crying, only hogs, only

hogs...

Heid E. Erdrich

LONG PIG

Girls like Peggy Lee,
bland, pink-faced
blondes, pale-lashed
and pug-nosed, those
girls made cheerleader,
student council, prom queen.
Sounds *jealous a little* — May be.
But now they've farrowed forth
four or five tow-headed young
to boar-broad farm husbands,
and learned to love guns and God.
Now they lean into their bones so cleanly,
not a lick of meat keeps up the cute.
All that flesh was like a lush suit that got
all their wants met. Sounds *cannibal* — May be.
Maybe love's suckling piglet
wicked out what sweet fat
contained that squealing girl.
Sounds *not fair* — May be.
Maybe their love feeds like any human love:
It renders, scalds, boils down
to everything but the oink.
More than my love —
Less than oink, just O,
and ink.

Louise Erdrich

PIG

The wisest cultures on earth
will have nothing to do with me
because they know
I am almost human:
I proliferate beyond my means
and bite before I'm bitten.
I eat anything and sleep in shit
if I must, though I am clean.
I incubate death in my gut.
I am intelligent
but my flesh is sweet.
If you want your billions
to be graves for my billions
go ahead.
But the wise ones know
there should only be a few of us,
for we are helpless
before our need
to devour this delicious world.

Martín Espada

CADA PUERCO TIENE SU SÁBADO
— For Angel Guadalupe

Cada puerco tiene su sábado,
Guadalupe would say.
Every pig has his Saturday.

Guadalupe remembered a Saturday
in Puerto Rico, when his uncle Chungo
clanked a pipe across the skull of a shrieking pig,
wrestled the staggering blood-slick beast
before the flinching children.
Chungo set the carcass ablaze
to burn the bristles off the skin.
Guadalupe dreamt for years about
that flaming pig. Of his uncle,
he would only say:
Cada puerco tiene su sábado.
And Chungo died, diving into the ocean,
an artery bursting his head.

I remember a Saturday
on Long Island,
when my father dug a pit
for the pig roast,
and neighbors spoke prophecy
of dark invasion
beneath the growl of lawnmowers.
I delivered the suckling pig,
thirty pounds in my arms,
cradled in a plastic bag
with trotters protruding
and flies bouncing off the snout,
skinned by a farmer
who did not know
the crunch of cuero.
My father cursed the lost skin,

cursed the rain filling the pit,
cursed the oven too small for the pig,
cursed the pig he beheaded
on the kitchen counter,
cursed his friends who left
before the pig was brown.

Amid the dented beer cans
leaning back to back,
I stayed with my cursing father.
I was his accomplice;
witnesses in doorways saw me
carrying the body through the streets.
I ate the pig too,
jaw grinding thick pork
like an outfielder's tobacco.
The farmer told me
the pig's name: Ichabod.

Cada puerco tiene su sábado.

DSS DREAM

I dreamed
the Department of Social Services
came to the door and said:
"We understand
you have a baby,
a goat and a pig living here
in a two-room apartment.
This is illegal.
We have to take the baby away,
unless you eat the goat."

"The pig's OK?" I asked.
"The pig's OK," they said.

Jane Gentry

PORTRAIT OF THE ARTIST AS A WHITE PIG

At sunset on a November day, the world unrolls
itself beside the Western Kentucky Parkway.
Gilded in sunlight, bronze as a baby shoe,
the dead leaves burn on the trees, red, gold,
black, spread rich as an Oriental rug.
Green flames of side-lit cedars burnish all.

Then over the short horizon appears the hero,
alien as brontosaurus, strange,
but of a multitude: white pigs,
a field full, eating, all snouts
to the ground they've rooted up, plowed
like furrows in the cognac-colored light.
That earth should take the form of this
strange beast, should eat itself and shift
into this shape! The bows of their backs
gold-leafed: snout and mouth to golden earth,
as hungry as one breath for the next.
Unnatural as Midas' kingdom
in the sideways sun, what other
brutes could translate this
bright dirt? This heavy
light? These showers of gold?

Jane Graham George

SWINE JUDGING, DAKOTA COUNTY FAIR

Plaid-shirt farmboys with bale-strong
arms leaning on the metal corrals,
grandmas, other pigs and handlers,
all watch breathlessly as a small
teen-aged girl and her black, white-
belted pig stand waiting for the judge
who speaks as though he hails
from one of the finest salons
in Europe, literary, I mean,
as if awarding the Prix Goncourt,
enunciating each honeyed word.
"Folks, this young lady does not poke or prod,
is at one with her charming Hampshire hog.
4-H or not, this is equanimity."
Though she really does look like Athena,
it isn't quite like hitting a home run
or sinking a putt from an improbable distance
which is why, once the judge awards the blue ribbon,
there's no arm pumping, no prom-spinning in place.
Something about a hog does bring you right back to earth.

Donald Hall

EATING THE PIG

Twelve people, most of us strangers, stand in a room
in Ann Arbor, drinking Cribari from jars.
Then two young men, who cooked him,
carry him to the table
on a large square of plywood: his body
striped, like a tiger cat's, from the basting,
his legs long, much longer than a cat's,
and the striped hide as shiny as vinyl.

Now I see his head, as he takes his place
at the center of the table,
his wide pig's head; and he looks like the *javelina*
that ran in front of the car, in the desert outside Tucson,
and I am drawn to him, my brother the pig,
with his large ears cocked forward,
with his tight snout, with his small ferocious teeth
in a jaw propped open
by an apple. How bizarre, this raw apple clenched
in a cooked face! Then I see his eyes,
his eyes cramped shut, his no-eyes, his eyes like X's
in a comic strip, when the character gets knocked out.

This afternoon they read directions
from a book: *The eyeballs must be removed
or they will burst during roasting.* So they hacked them out.
"I nearly fainted," says someone.
"I never fainted before, in my whole life."
Then they gutted the pig and stuffed him,
and roasted him five hours, basting the long body.

༄

Now we examine him, exclaiming, and we marvel at him —
but no one picks up a knife.

Then a young woman cuts off his head.
It comes off so easily, like a detachable part.
With sudden enthusiasm we dismantle the pig,
we wrench his trotters off, we twist them
at shoulder and hip, and they come off so easily.
Then we cut open his belly and pull the skin back.

For myself, I scoop a portion of left thigh,
moist, tender, falling apart, fat, sweet.
We forage like an army starving in winter
that crosses a pass in the hills and discovers
a valley of full barns —
cattle fat and lowing in their stalls,
bins of potatoes in root cellars under white farmhouses,
barrels of cider, onions, hens squawking over eggs —
and the people nowhere, with bread still warm in the oven.

Maybe, south of the valley, refugees pull their carts
listening for Stukas or elephants, carrying
bedding, pans, and silk dresses,
old men and women, children, deserters, young wives.

No, we are here, eating the pig together.

       ಕ

In ten minutes, the destruction is total.

His tiny ribs, delicate as birds' feet, lie crisscrossed.
Or they are like crosshatching in a drawing,
lines doubling and redoubling on each other.

Bits of fat and muscle
mix with stuffing alien to the body,
walnuts and plums. His skin, like a parchment bag
soaked in oil, is pulled back and flattened,
with ridges and humps remaining, like a contour map,
like the map of a defeated country.

The army consumes every blade of grass in the valley,
every tree, every stream, every village,
every crossroad, every shack, every book, every graveyard.

His intact head
swivels around, to view the landscape of body
as if in dismay.

"For sixteen weeks I lived. For sixteen weeks
I took into myself nothing but the milk of my mother
who rolled on her side for me,
for my brothers and sisters. Only five hours roasting,
and this body so quickly dwindles away to nothing."

※

By itself, isolated on this plywood,
among this puzzle of foregone possibilities,
his intact head seems to want affection.
Without knowing that I will do it,
I reach out and scratch his jaw,
and I stroke him behind his ears,
as if he might suddenly purr from his cooked head.

"When I stroke your pig's ears,
and scratch the striped leather of your jowls,
the furrow between the sockets of your eyes,
I take into myself, and digest,
wheat that grew between
the Tigris and the Euphrates rivers.

"And I take into myself the flint carving tool,
and the savannah, and hairs in the tail
of Eohippus, and fingers of bamboo,
and Hannibal's elephant, and Hannibal,
and everything that lived before us, everything born,
exalted, and dead, and historians who carved in the Old Kingdom
when the wall had not heard about China."

I speak these words
into the ear of the Stone Age pig, the Abraham
pig, the ocean pig, the Achilles pig,
and into the ears
of the fire pig that will eat our bodies up.

"Fire, brother and father,
twelve of us, in our different skins, older and younger,
opened your skin together
and tore your body apart, and took it
into our bodies."

SOWS I HAVE KNOWN

After watching the *Wizard of Oz*
for the first time
what kept this girl tossing
was Dorothy's tumble
into the sow's pen.

I knew those pigs.
In the barn
they slept in superior comfort
snuffling their flat noses
acting entitled
in ways the cows
and horses didn't dare.
And the sow.
Too knowing.
Too certain.
Too proud
of her too human teeth.

She haunts me decades later,
a cloven old testament matriarch
willing to consume her children,
and me, and mine.

Han-shan (Cold Mountain)

#72

Pigs devour dead human flesh
humans savor dead pig guts
pigs don't mind human stink
humans say pork smells fine
throw dead pigs in the river
bury human bodies deep
if they ever stop eating each other
lotuses will bloom in boiling soup

— *Translated by Bill Porter*

Margaret Hasse

BEAUTY PARADING MAIN STREET

Miss Custom Combine rides atop a float
like a slender statuette, her hair sheaves
of golden wheat. Along comes kicking
a small majorette in a lampshade skirt
and red underpants who twirls the bone
of her baton for the marching band
to follow. Next, on a platform decorated
to promote *the other white meat,*
Miss Pork Queen, slim as a bacon strip,
burns her bare shoulders in the August heat.

Sharing the passing throne, sandwiched
between planes of a wire pen,
the sow stands foursquare in silhouette
revealing her broad satin side,
her thick neck that needs no string
of tiny pearls, her muscular
stifle, the juggling clubs of her giant hams,
swags of her udder hung with swollen teats
each one pink-tipped as a candy cigarette —
female flesh given the blue-ribbon prize
not just for trim, but for titanic size.

John Southall Hatcher

PIG THOUGHTS AT NOON

a vegetarian stroked at noon behind my ears
mumbled about my being bred for death (his pun),
but his thoughts were elsewhere

among feathers, furs, rare flaming symmetry
and outspread wings, not me;

for though my soul dwells beyond swift stallions
and above the tree-couched cat
I am groomed for termination
and no one mourns my passing.

He means well, I suppose —
my friend the vegetarian —
but when he tries to find comparisons for me
his mind wanders to the puma, the cheetah, the jaguar
(the sum of whose lifetime thoughts
I could formulate on one hoof);

socratically he tries to penetrate
my crude surfaces
but is stopped by the shadows of things:

he cannot caress my short hair, bulk, snout,
cannot remove himself from reflexive imagery —
the stuck pig still squeals
no pearls are cast before me
I am symbol for greed and
things remote from godliness
forbidden as vile to some
but devoured at every part
feet, brains, joints, entrails.

So it is that I
become each of you

and am your metaphor —
what you seek as you peek behind the surfaces,
for who has sensed the nobility in my pig heart
and has caught the glint in my eyes
can ponder the beginning of the universe
and probe the heart of man.

John Southall Hatcher

PIG SONG

Si you creyera que mi repuesta sería
a persona que pudiera hablar con el agricultor,
este cerdito nuna más charlaría;
pero, porque tu no puedes convencerle de
que un cerdo ha hablado contigo,
voy a decirte unas cosas en confianza.
— Juan Valdez de Santa Toledo

Let us go then, you and I,
where the field yields to the sty
like a "See Rock City" poster on a stable;
let us go through certain half-erected roosts
where some ducklings or a goose
speaks of sleepless nights in one-perch cheep chicken pens
and barnyards swept with sins;
roosts that reek with stale fowl smell
and birds pell mell
that make you want to yell some swelling question . . .
come on, now, ask me, "What is it?"
No? . . . well, let's take a walk.

In the sty they come and go
speaking of the rodeo.

The moist hay odor drifts along the gutters,
the green smell that steps up and mutters,
licks my back in the corners where it itches,
lingers among the trough and sputters,
passes through the farmer's kitchen who,
thinking his wife fast asleep at last,
reads lewd magazines to escape her bitching.

And indeed there will be time
to tell you of the smell that glides along the grass
and drifts along the gutters;

There will be time, there will be time
to make a squeak to greet the squealers I will meet;
and time for all the playful things
with all the luscious treats to swallow;
time for you and time for me,
and time yet for a hundred incisions
and for a hundred divisions
and being served with toast and tea.

In the sty they come and go
speaking of the rodeo.

And indeed there will be time
to blurt out, "Eat a peach!" or "Eat a pear!"
Time to slide into the mud kersplat
like falling in a jello vat.
(The roosters will say, "My, his legs are getting fat!")

My double chin, my rounding rump
my shoulders bulging in a clump
(The ducks will mutter, "But how his belly is getting plump!")
Do I dare
get up from the mud?
In a minute there is time
for incisions and divisions to make a ham of stud.

No! I am not a fierce wild boar, nor was meant to be;
am an old stud hog, one that will do
to swell a sow, start a litter or two,
no doubt with an easy tool,
deferential, glad to be of use,
chubby, stout, ridiculous,
full of pounds, but a bit obtuse;
at times, indeed, almost obscene —
almost, at times, a piggy bank.

I grow round ... I grow round ...
I shall be measured pound for pound.

Shall I venture to the trough, do I dare to stuff with starches?
I shall dine on low-cal tubers and go on diet marches.
I have heard the farmers talking each to each.
I hope they will not come for me.
I have seen them riding their large white mares,
combing the white-haired mane for the fair
where the judges weigh and then compare.

We have lingered in the corners of the pen,
amid the mire, slime, and swill strewn through the sty
Till human voices *"So o o o ey!"* and we die.

John Southall Hatcher

THE MIGHTY ANGLO-SAXON HOG UPRISING

Yorkshire, Hampshire,   Berkshire and Duroc,
pigs all file,   brave boars together.
Battle-hard Sidney,   their swinely swift liege pig
to his war-porkers spoke,   to his stout horde began:
        "Famed shield-hogs,   offspring of ealdors,
fierce battle-times   in yore-days many
have we abided   the ringing of hand-swords,
the crashing of heirlooms,   adorned battle-blades,
now to us is come   our renowned victory-time.
Endure it we must   the shedding of boar blood
for kinsmen, our brothers,   alone in the ground;
better to avenge   one warrior well
than sadly to mourn   ten thousand a lifetime
without battle-sweat."
        Thus from afar   could their loathed-one see
these pig-troops assembled,   the war-ready bands.
From barrows and burgs   they watched hog-hordes heave high
bright banners and ash-spears,   gold shields and bold blades
and stout battle-weeds;   they heard grunting and squealing,
with reason they trembled,   with swine-fear they dreaded
the resolute boar-lords,   the hog-rush to come.
        Then as I have heard   in the gabled sty-hall
spoke the famed of the battle-shoats,   the high-minded Lothar
the choicest of trough-lads: "Hear now my mind-thoughts,
valor-clad war-hogs,   for the gem of the heavens
now nears the hilltops;   not longer may we
abide here in peace.   Sidney our liege lord
has need of our brave deeds,   glory-work in warfare
with the two-footed foe.   He it was who gave us,
the high-sitting pork lord,   these morsels for munching
and burnished gold nose rings.   Now has the time come
when our corn-giver god   has need of our swine strength,
kin-pigs together.   Now will we barter
loaned-life for glory,   win fame for the far-herds
and acorns for rooting."

                Then were the swift ones
warlike to see there   eager for battle.
Straight-way the terror   was made known to the pork-foes,
the wretched ones,   as I have heard;
throughout the middle-yard   was told to all
of proud-marching boar-bands,   the war-ready swine,
of Chester White, Landrace,   Poland China and Hereford,
of Large Black and Tamworth,   breeders and porkers,
all shining in war-gear.   Not as in yore-days
when hog-hearts were humbled,   but stepping with snouts high
they went westward and eastward,   amid forests and walled-burgs,
near nesses and high-halls   and farm dwellings many.
With vengeance and hot ire   they broke loose the pen-bonds,
marched through the wide plains   and righted old wrongs.
            Those were good pigs   who quick comfort gave
to Sidney their leader,   the wise lord of oinkers,
and Lothar the young shoat   who good counsel gave.
Grim were the trough-friends,   scathers to keepers,
hard to the hog-foes   who fled from the land.

Robert Hedin

SAINTE-FOY

Up in the Pyrenees they killed
Their animals with stones,
And before that
By running their herds
Into the blazing air of these foothills.
Here at the church of Sainte-Foy,
The blood of those animals
Comes back night after night.
It comes back as dust
On the old stonecutter,
The Basque who climbs every sundown
Up the long rocky path.
It comes back as earth and stone,
As hard chunks of mortar
And clay I pull from the walls
And smell what is Sainte-Foy,
A silence so deep I could stay here
And breathe this cold forever,
All this wet uncut stone
That is Sainte-Foy —
A vow I take deep, and break
As my headlights go on,
And see in the graveyard out back,
Snout buried in mud and clay,
A hog big enough for slaughter,
A loose sow that grunts once
At my lights, and doesn't move.
She stands there as I turn,
Her ears and pink back steaming
In the cold, feeding on the dead
And what the dead push up.

Robert Hedin

TORNADO

The last time any of us saw Gustafson's prize sow
She was rising over the floodlights
Of the poultry barns, pedaling off into a sky
Dark with wreckage.
                        If ever a sow was beautiful
It was she — 1200 pounds of blue-ribbon pork
Rooted down deep on her wallow, her whole body
Lit with gold chaff.
                      By morning she was famous.
And when we found Gustafson, he was rocking
In the middle of his pigsty,
Staring west toward the county line.
And all we could hear was the rain
And its thin ticking against the leaves,
The empty swill pail still vibrating in his hands.

Tom Hennen

SUNLIGHT AFTER THE PIG YARD FLOOD

Washed up
On the mud like a lifeboat
The old sow blinks.
Close to her belly her little ones
Make the snoring noises of happy survivors.

William Heyen

PIG NOTES

EMPIRICISM

At the Orleans County Fair I was looking into the pigsty when its proprietor threw in a pailful of soggy vegetables and spoiled fruit. The sty's several inhabitants snorted and pushed and rolled in muck, competing for this fare. I heard a child who was looking on say, "Yeeks, what pigs, no wonder they call them pigs."

UTILITARIANISM

In another sty, a pig was snouting around a perfect pigtoy. What toy couldn't be chewed or eaten or knocked out of the pen? What was safe and indestructible and heavy enough to provide pig exercise? What would roll when pushed as though alive? The pig was snouting around a bowling ball.

O SAGES OF CONCORD

At Brook Farm in 1841 — I see him as though in a movie — Nathaniel Hawthorne is staring down into a pen, meditating on several of the community swine: "I suppose it is the knowledge that these four companions are doomed to die within two or three weeks that gives them a sort of awfulness in my conception. It makes me contrast their sudden gross substance of fleshy life with the nothingness speedily to come.... They appear more a mystery the longer one gazes at them. It seems as if there were an important meaning to them, if one could but find it out."

Nathaniel is baffled and intrigued by the evanescence of pighood — he senses some kind of swine transcendentalism — but you and I, too far from the ideas of Brook Farm, are not particularly interested in these grunters. We know that pigs mean what they are, that what they are and what they provide — their own utilitarianism — are the same, whether or not we can say it. Lights, camera, action: knuckles, chops, bacon.

THE MUSE

In another sty, a boar was rooting in slop beneath its mate's body. Having had her fill earlier, she was sleeping, but the boar kept snouting beneath her body, at one point almost rolling her over. He didn't care about her own plans for the afternoon. And that snuffling noise made us think he felt close to discovering a field of truffles. But she kept at her sleeping, and he never managed, this time, to turn her over or even get her attention.

Jim Heynen

TORNADO ALERT

That night
against a copper sky there rose
a body, large and dark,
extending land to cloud.

On the dusty stack of last
year's hay I sat and watched it
lumber nearer, wavering, frayed,
and almost letting loose
to stringy clouds,
then tightening toward
human form. Steadily,
it looked at me,
and I knew it was a woman.

For all I knew of women
was there, the mystery I dreamed
beneath the flowing skirts of aunts,
the fleshy angles
of teen-age girls —
and now a broad hip
swaying, a lithesome
fluid rhythm
that was always foreign,
always close to my imagining —
a song translated to the sky
and one with it.

From all directions
came her silence breathing in
my breath, a feeling heavy
from inside that could have been
a wish to leap into
her grand revolving.
My hesitation broke

her silence into laughter,
shattering the oats.
I felt the urge the fence
posts followed leaping
from their dull lives in earth
to dance the sky,

or at least
to let my clothing go
the way the corn
in all its ordered rows
let go its leaves and seed to be
one with swirling cloud.

Half-mad with yearning,
half-crazed by fear,
I burrowed down to root myself
in hay. And then

from near the hog house
a sow ascended,
a wingless flight
into the guttural roar of mud and dust,
its thick form turning
slowly, its snout agape,
its short legs pedaling air —
a crazy celebration, her joining,
as if by choice, the sky
hilarious with debris.

First rain,
then the stinging sky,
struck my face.
All her darkness was upon me.
All her rage.

The pig was gone.
I heard my own unwilling
scream of terror

and turned face-down, clawing
like a rodent trapped in hail.
With no choice but to live it out,
I scratched and writhed, prying
the stubborn sea
of hay, my only hope
a burial. Submerging
so deep that sight and sound
were gone,
I lived
the single smell
of molding, musty hay.

Whoever it was survived
climbed through my chest,
and I stood upright
into torrents of friendly rain
on the fire of torn skin.

The bristling sow
weaved through my mind.
Somewhere,
I imagined her
still skirmishing with filthy air,
still turning over and over
in a sky of wreckage.
I heard the rescue sirens,
frail strands of sound.
I saw the sad, disheveled farmyard.
I saw the waxen faces of my frightened
parents peering from the cellar.

And I laughed,
already denying those reports
of finding, 30 miles east,
stomach sliced by the free-wheeling
ploughshares of the sky,
the haughty, grunting, earthy sow.

Jim Heynen

DURING SPRING FLOODS

The cows stayed
on high ground or,
when they had to,
swam with the current
and usually made it.
Horses too.

But pigs couldn't wallow
in so much water:
their forefeet came up too high
and caught
on their thick jowls.
They could swim for a hundred yards
or so, looking no worse
than large muskrats, until
they completely cut their throats,
then sank under the current of blood
passing over them.

Jim Heynen

FARROWING PEN

Last night
you snapped at my hand,
old bristly woman.
Now you ignore me,
don't even hear sparrows
chattering in the eaves.

Who could believe this —
the old sow with her frothy snout
shaping a dam out of straw,
mouthfuls of straw, each
edged into place for this
magnificent cradle,
this smooth-prowed boat,
this sow-nest!

It has only begun.
She falls in,
lies still as an egg
until contractions begin,
a breeze on a hedge,
bristles rippling, vagina
swelling and splitting with blood.
But still the ease,
slow commotion of birth.
The small pig arrives
and the sparrows never stop singing.

No one here is surprised,
not even the newborn
stepping out of its birth-sac,
the small ears unravelling
smooth as a conch
to hear its own life in straw,

the sparrow's singing,
the sow's slow breathing.

Does she remember
the first task —
to straddle the umbilical cord,
break free and leave it
drying on the straw,
and to move on, circling the nest,
until the mouth, as now,
touches flesh,
and is home?

Jim Heynen

SOMETIMES A SOW

Sometimes a sow
couldn't have her young.
They'd catch
in the tight gate
of her womb
and she'd lie heaving
towards death.

When I was ten
I learned a trick
to get them out —
a metal hook
in my hand
into the birth channel
shoulder deep
to find
the small snout.
I'd slip the hook
under the chin,
hold my breath,
and pull.

Sometimes
the wish-bone jaw
shattered
and the pig died,
but when it worked
the release was sudden —
a small form
wet in my hands.

At the sound of life
the sow would sigh
her jowled sigh
and I would sigh

and put the pig
bleeding
to her teats.

Bill Holm

PIG

I have lain in the mud all day
Softening the bristles on my back,
Combing my ears on the box-elder tree
Till they stand up straight and pink.
Now I am going into the darkness —
To prepare for love.

Bill Holm

OLD SOW ON THE ROAD
— For Walt Gislason

Thirty below. A hundred miles from home
the Buick throws a rod. Dead.
An hour later, I'm headed south
away from Paynesville in a truck.
A half mile out an old sow sits
on broken haunches in the middle
of the road. We stop. Maybe
fell off a stock truck: nobody
saw her in the iced-up mirror.
She swivels on that broken back, a pink
lazy Susan turning on the yellow line.
Ice blue light, gun barrel pavement,
pink nose, snow, snow, more snow.
Airy colors for such a monster painting.
Windows iced tight, heater purrs loud,
but by God, I hear the howling
of that old sow, snout rotating, a double
barreled gun aimed straight at me.
And that face! That face said everything
I'll ever say until I'm either dead
or alive as that sow at that moment
wanted so badly to be.

Ted Hughes

THE PIG
— Excerpt from *What Is The Truth?*

The Pig that ploughs the orchard with her nose
Returns
Strutting in her tiny tutu.

The Pig that lies unearthed out there, a giant potato,
Or snores in the straw, an eyeless, legless
Water-bed of wobble and quake,
Can sprint faster than you can.

The sow fallen out there, cratered in mud,
Like the circus fat lady
Fallen off her tightrope, is not happy.
She wants to be a real lady.

The Pig that peers up at you, with blubbery nose
And eyes red from weeping
Wants to be you.

And the lean weaner, with his sawed-off shotgun grin,
Squints his little Judas eye at you.
Oh he's wicked! He burps laughter!
A flea
Earthquakes the world of pig.
And he's splitting at the seams
To keep in the explosion of laughter.
The eyelids screw down tight, keeping it in.
He wants to be a naughty comedian.

The big boar has problems
With the battered swill-buckets of his ears.
He keeps trying to arrange them over his eyes
Like big poppy petals, but they're too floppy.
I know I'm no beauty, he says. I live for my children.

And the piglets, in elevens and thirteens,
Galloping like apples poured from a barrel,
Flogging themselves with their ears,
Trying to escape from their tails
Cry: Take us with you, take us with you.

All pine for the day they will be people.

Colette Inez

LITTLE PIG OF BEAUTY

Little pig of beauty sets the swine style
in the corner of her pen, too frail to breed,
moon-hued lashes, dainty trotters, all the rage
to other porkers grunting and barking
through summer-scented days of corn, zucchini,
beefsteak tomatoes ripening in tune
to her bright soprano squeal and the bass snuffle
of the suitor who overcomes her diffidence.
Then the blunt end of an ax put the kibosh on her bliss.
At dinner I said thanks to a second helping.
From the kitchen mirror flashed back a twitch
of snout, eyes screwed in their sockets
blinking watery blue.

John Janovy, Jr.

GOD LOVED PIGS
— Excerpt from *Conversations Between God and Satan*

God was beginning to think that maybe people were not such a good idea after all because the planets that still had only dinosaurs and trilobites and giant dragonflies seemed to be doing just fine, so that maybe when He got tired of watching velociraptor types chomping down on gentle herbivores, instead of killing them off with a big meteorite, He'd just see if He could evolve them into pigs of various sizes and shapes. "I like pigs," He said to Himself, and thought about the pleasure He felt when He was watching strange plants and animals evolve from other strange plants and animals, sort of like He'd created a circus over whose acts He had no control whatsoever.

"Birds," said Satan, reading God's mind and reminding Him of His own operating principles. "You can't make pigs out of velociraptors. You can only make birds."

"I forgot," said God; "pigs are made out of something else." God loved pigs because they were so honest and successful and, well, predictable. They simply acted like pigs, and even the various wild species He'd watched evolve out of some even-toed ancestor non-pig. All the pigs that had evolved out of their even-toed ancestors on millions of other planets also were great pigs and would probably have done just fine on Earth, even though they came in a variety of styles, sizes, and colors, including purple or iridescent chartreuse, depending on the galaxy. "You gotta admit it," said God; "pigs are one of my Universe's best products."

"It is amazing, isn't it," replied Satan; "that people act like pigs but pigs never act like people." She was reminding God of why they'd come to The Crescent Moon, namely, to talk about people, not about the good stuff like pigs.

Louis Jenkins

LEOTI

Great Grandpa Charlie thought he could get rich in America so he came to Leoti, Kansas in the 1880s. There was a fight going on over which town, Leoti or nearby Coronado, would be the county seat. Wyatt Earp and Bat Masterson came to help shoot it out. Everybody felt there was money to be made. At this time, also, they were killing off the buffalo. Charlie got a wagon and he gathered the bones of slaughtered buffalo to sell to be made into fertilizer, and the horns were made into buttons. By the time the bones were all gone he'd made enough to buy some land, get married and build a sod house. Great Grandpa didn't stay too many years. It was a hard place to farm, flat and hard as a gaming table, treeless and dusty. Leoti won the war and is still county seat and the only town in the county. After the fight everyone moved out of Coronado. At the courthouse we located Great Grandpa's settlement on the big county map. My wife said, "We could drive out there and have a picnic." The clerk said, "I wouldn't do that if I were you. They raise a lot of pigs out there nowadays."

Rodney Jones

THE EATING OF SWINE

I have learned sloppiness from an old sow
wallowing her ennui in the stinking lot,
a slow vessel filled with a thousand candles,
her whiskers matted with creek mud,
her body helpless to sweat the dull spirit.
I have wrestled the hindquarters of a young boar
while my father clipped each testicle
with a sharpened barlow knife, returning him,
good fish, to his watery, changed life.
And I have learned pleasure from a gilt
as she lay on her back, offering her soft belly
like a dog, the loose bowel of her throat
opening to warble the consonants of her joy.
I have learned lassitude, pride, stubbornness,
and greed from my many neighbors, the pigs.
I have gone with low head and slanted blue eyes
through the filthy streets, wary of the blade,
my whole life, a toilet or kitchen,
the rotting rinds, the wreaths of flies.
For the chicken, the cow, forgetfulness. Mindlessness
blesses their meat. Only the pigs are holy,
the rings of their snouts, their fierce, motherly indignation,
and their need always to fill themselves.
I remember a photograph. A sheriff had demolished
a still, spilling a hundred gallons of moonshine.
Nine pigs passed out in the shade of a mulberry tree.
We know pigs will accommodate
demons, run into rivers, drowning of madness.
They will devour drunks who fall in their way.
Like Christ, they will befriend their destroyers.
In the middle of winter I have cupped my hands
and held the large and pliable brain of a pig.
As the fires were heating the black kettles,
I have scrupulously placed my rifle between pigs' eyes
and with one clean shot loosened the slabs

of side-meat, the sausages that begin
with the last spasms of the trotters.
O dolphins of the barnyard, frolickers
in the gray and eternal muck, in all your parts
useful, because I have known you, this is the sage,
and salt, the sacrificial marker of pepper.
What pity should I feel, or gratitude, raising you
on my fork as all the dead shall be risen?

DEMONS

Three little pigs
shining in their pen
is how it began.
I fed them
a mix of milk and grain,
potato peels and table scraps
soured in buckets.
I slopped it into
the rough wooden trough.
Because I was a kid
I laughed at their hunger
making mock snorts
shouting a long
drawn out "Sooo-ee".

Larger,
less charming,
no longer the pigs
of storybooks,
their hunger
outgrew their pen.
They escaped
more and more often.
They snapped at my thighs
as I herded them home.
They grew possessed;
their snouts could lift bricks.
Sometimes I found them
eating our garbage
and once
I found one
deep in the woods
gorging on the ripe
corpse of a calf.
It made me sick to see it.

A butcher was hired
who came and shot them.
One of the pigs
took the bullet
into its soft brain
and raced
a straight line
out of the farm yard
crossing a field of alfalfa
up and over a long hill,
following its own trajectory
for at least a mile
before dying
in the neighbor's oats.

Years later,
slowly turning the pages
of a book,
the memory
of that pig's dying
coursed through me
once more.
Dostoyevsky's men,
possessed by thoughts,
pointed by hungers,
died like the pigs
in the Bible. And
my forearms bristled as
I realized the demons
Dostoyevsky made
were the words
on which I fed.

Susan Deborah King

AMBIVALENCE

That some are pink,
though adulterated
by bristles of black;
that they grunt and snort,
snuffle, snarf, scarf;
that they are smart;
that they lead with their snouts
and are on the hoof
except when pooped;
that they are amped
about being fat,
are on intimate terms with dirt
and sport a spiral tail –
all these aspects appeal.
I smile at sows suckling
slobbering piglets, two long rows.
I'm a fan of *Charlotte's Web*
and bacon. So why, if I'm partial
to all these parts, can't I be happy
with the whole?

Is it because our race took a turn
for the worse when we buried
our bodies' animal knowing
to "get ahead" and I got swept along
like that expelled Gerasene demon horde
stampeding over the cliff or got herded
into a sty with those associating swine
with gluttons, Jews, floozies, cops,
into the *minyan* declaring them
not kosher, unfit?

I like the sound of *oink*.
I'd like to call *Soo-E!*
at the top of my lungs,

and it would be fun
to squeal in delight
and not on the run from a knife.
But at troughs running with slop,
the stench alone, I simply recoil.
Maybe I'm not as cool
as I'd like to think I am
with being in the body after all.
Maybe, unlike the prodigal, I haven't
fully come to myself. Could I
ever really let myself *wallow*,
let appetite go hog wild?

Galway Kinnell

SAINT FRANCIS AND THE SOW

The bud
stands for all things,
even those things that don't flower,
for everything flowers, from within, of self-blessing;
though sometimes it is necessary
to reteach a thing its loveliness,
to put a hand on its brow
of the flower
and retell it in words and in touch
it is lovely
until it flowers again from within, of self-blessing;
as Saint Francis
put his hand on the creased forehead
of the sow, and told her in words and in touch
blessing of earth on the sow, and the sow
began remembering all down her thick length,
from the earthen snout all the way
through the fodder and slops to the spiritual curl of the tail,
from the hard spininess spiked out from the spine
down through the great broken heart
to the sheer blue milken dreaminess spurting and shuddering
from the fourteen teats into the fourteen mouths sucking and
        blowing beneath them:
the long perfect loveliness of sow.

Galway Kinnell

THE SOW PIGLET'S ESCAPE

When the little sow piglet squirmed free,
Gus and I ran her all the way down to the swamp
and lunged and floundered and fell full-length
on our bellies stretching for her — and got her! —
and lay there all three shining with swamp slime —
she yelping, I laughing, Gus — it was then I knew
he would die soon — gasping and gasping.
She made her second escape on the one day
when she was just big enough to dig an escape hole
and still small enough to squeeze through it.
Every day for the next week I took a bucket of meal
to her plot of rooted-up ground in the woods,
until one day there she was, waiting for me,
the wild beast evidently all mealed out of her.
She trotted over and let me stroke her back
and, dribbling corn down her chin, put up her little worried face
as if to remind me not to forget to recapture her —
though, really, a pig's special alertness to death
ought to have told her: in Sheffield the *dolce vita*
leads to the Lyndonville butcher. But when I seized her
she wriggled hard and cried, *wee wee wee,* all the way home.

William Kloefkorn

TWO POEMS FROM
ALVIN TURNER AS FARMER

    1

So pshaw! the hogs went loose again,
And I can't blame a women for saying
She is sick to the death of manure.
At a time like that even the mind
Goes muddied. (But she did very well,
That woman, hip-deep in muck,
Circling those hogs like a snake hunt
Closing in. And all the while
Going to the mud on her apron
To wipe the mud off her hands.
Manure, she calls it, and I don't argue.)
At such a time
The lifting of a single thread
Unhems the world.
The price of corn is up.
Hogs are down.
The next thing you know
The government will place a tax
On prayer. All this, and more,
As we change our socks
And put on new faces for supper.

    2

friends that
fresh-braised pork
you're licking chops
to was on the
hoof a week ago
rooting rubbish
with the same
nostrils i chose
to fire the rifle bullets

into that act being
only one of god's
manifold mysterious
ways for which
on this november day
we all should probably
give thanks
amen!

William Kloefkorn

LUDI JR., AS THE HIRED HAND, PAYS DEARLY FOR WHAT HE IS PAID FOR

beginning the task spick and span
spitting like a lumberjack
into the cups of his bare calloused hands
ludi jr jumps over the gate in a single stride
to confront face to snout
the hog that he has been hired
to stalk and bring to his back and bind

but after more than one lunge
after half a dozen frenzied dives
the palms the arms the boots the bib
hang heavy as sashweights with dung

and he takes a break
several long deep deliberate breaths
before plunging in again

the hog meanwhile
wide and low and apparently immobile
watching the hired hand resting
watching him.

until with a fresh vigor
ludi jr begins all over again
hogshit and corncobs and mudchips
like the devil's own
dark flurry of divots
storming the pen
neither hog nor man
willing to back down
the sounds from them
frequent and brief and gutteral

the face now of the hired man
aslop with that square of space
where only a second earlier
the hog had been
a crust of hair only
in the hired man's fisted hand

and he takes a second break
this time not simply to breathe
but to think things over

while the hog
wide and low and all at once again
apparently immobile

guards his ground
grunting watching

and here is what the hired man knows
but cannot think:
the essence of hog

in the boots hog
in the hair hog
in the nose hog
in the eyes
down the back
between the lips
against the tongue
adrift all up and down the spine
hinged in the knuckles
in the elbows in the knees
in the bend and snap of the ankles

hog

knowing but not thinking that no word
not even hog hog hog hog hog
can backflush the bowel that is truly hog

like brother cannot itself
as either sound or squibble
be what the brother knows
under the skin in the bone
to be

that no smell however stout
can do it either
no snort no grunt no squeal
however deep and short
however shrill
the syllable

yet something in the belly
bristles with the same blood:
that will hot and defiant
not now or ever to be laid hold of

which means that ludi jr
no less than god
must earn his keep:
must become the essence of hog
before he has the right of blood
to bind the feet

and when all of that has come to pass
and the snout is seized
and the head is forced back
and the quaint taut throbbing throat
gushes red

must drink as if elixir from the very well
he dreamed and planned and dug himself

and filled

Ted Kooser

WILD PIGS

There's four square miles of timber, mostly oak,
just north of here; the only stand of trees
much bigger than a wind-break up or down
the county, and it's thick as thatch, so thick
two fellows shot themselves by accident
just getting through the brush along the road.
The place is full of deer, and pheasants, and quail
like swarms of horseflies in a dairy barn.
And, listen up: they say there's pigs in there,
wild pigs, the size of hunting dogs, with tusks
that'll snap a fellow's shin-bone like a twig.
The story goes that in the Civil War
some farmer from Missouri drove them here
to keep the army from conscripting them.
They say he fed them acorns through the war,
and when he went to drive them home again
in '65 they wouldn't go. No Sir;
they liked those acorns! Oh, he tried and tried
to get them out; hired herders, set a fire,
shot some of them for something, God knows why.
Although he caught a few of them, some stayed
and multiplied, and got as wild as wolves.
They're up there now, if anybody'd look.

Kathryn Kysar

WHEN PIGS FLY: KURT'S DIARY

April 10, 1984
The weight of my jealousy
is unbearable. Bones behind
my eyes crack, and I wonder
who will stop these daffodils
from changing into ants.
My grandfather taught me
to eat the shells of hard boiled
eggs, but I want to hear plastic
turtles blooming from my ears.

April 12, 1984
The wind is starting to blow.
A storm moves in, then claps
of thunder burst over my roof.
I am inside, clutching a bottle.
The stove hasn't worked for days.
I am hungry for burgers, loaves
and fishes, more beer, you.

April 14, 1984
The wolves locked up
after they delivered the mail.
I cannot move my left arm, and now
flying pigs wing the bathroom air.
I've forgotten how to survive.

The cockroaches are singing again
in the kitchen, a regular Kansas chorus
of radon and lead. I find
your message hidden under
the clothes still stinking of vomit.
You will not be coming home.

Julie Landsman

PROPERTY VALUES

Retired Professor Lucas sat on a splintered porch surrounded by his city yard. A year before, this same Professor had lost his wife Belinda, long ill and long weakening.

Now bereft, as Delilah, one of his two pot-bellied pigs, had died. Samson, the other pig, and the professor mourned, their world shrunken by lost love. Neighbors built fences to keep the smell and squeal from their gardens.

In January Prof. Lucas brought a new pig home, delighted with her rotund happiness. Samson took to Eve, nuzzled her around the rattletrap house. "For Sale" signs appeared up and down the block as cold magnified the baby's shrieks. Next door, they scurried to close a deal by April before buyers would get a whiff of pig.

Prof. Lucas was unaware of his neighbors' flight, and if they voiced objections, he glittered tears, whispered how his Belinda and Delilah had passed on so now he had only Samson and the latest, Eve.

In June, rocking on the old glider with one pig on either side of his body he muffled his lonely life with snout, with belly on belly.

Prof. Lucas did not notice delight in the eyes of a newly arrived toddler who stared down at him from her bedroom window, did not hear her chuckle at the snuggling tangle just below.

Kristin Laurel

RESCUE

Some animals are more equal than others.
— George Orwell, *Animal Farm*

Next to an overturned semi trailer,
firemen prod away pigs with brooms.
My helicopter lands in the middle of the highway.

The truck, packed with pigs on the way
to the slaughterhouse, turned a corner
and flipped the trailer when the pigs
shifted their weight.

A Mexican man is strapped to the stretcher,
a bleeding gash on his head,
a piece of his right ear missing,
I ask, *Were you knocked unconscious?*
He's mute at first, then yells *No Inglais!*
above the noise of a hundred squealing pigs.

I've been told pigs squeal about anything
by my brother-in-law, the hog inseminator.
He loves his job, says *I work with tits and clits all day.*

They've got a right to squeal today.

Pigs, I once read, are what the Nazis called the millions of Jews,
Poles, and other human beings loaded into boxcars,
branded and exterminated.

In America, Mexicans die roasting in boxcars
trying to get here to pick our vegetables,
butcher our animals, do grunt work.

There's nothing pretty about it. But
I still eat my holiday ham, my pinto beans, my bacon.

We pack the patient into the back of the chopper.
He is scared to death, will be *just fine*, but
who's going to save the pigs?

Blades of grass bend beneath the force of spinning rotors.
Down below, a hundred pigs still squeal.
Flesh-colored snouts and hooves squirm

and wave between the trailer's metal bars
while the pigs on top trample and crush
the pigs on the bottom.

David Lee

LOADING A BOAR

We were loading a boar, a goddam mean big sonofabitch and he jumped out of the pickup four times and tore out my stockracks and rooted me in the stomach and I fell down and he bit John on the knee and he thought it was broken and so did I and the boar stood over in the far corner of the pen and watched us and John and I just sat there tired and Jan laughed and brought us a beer and I said, "John it aint worth it, nothing's going right and I'm feeling half dead and haven't wrote a poem in ages and I'm ready to quit it all," and John said, "shit, young feller, you aint got started yet and the reason's cause you trying to do it outside yourself and aint looking in and if you wanna by god write pomes you gotta write pomes about what you know and not about the rest and you can write about pigs and that boar and Jan and you and me and the rest and there aint no way you're gonna quit," and we drank beer and smoked, all three of us, and finally loaded that mean bastard and drove home and unloaded him and he bit me again and I went in the house and got out my paper and pencils and started writing and found out John he was right.

David Lee

CULTURE

So Aeneas walked up the Tiber until he found
a sow
she had a litter of thirty pigs
and he knew it was a sign
that would be the place

Where'd he go to get a boar?

No, it was a myth.

But where'd he get his boar?

He didn't. He killed the sow on the site
and sacrificed
her to the gods for marking the place

You goddam stupid sonofabitch how come you telling me stories
like that I'm busy I haven't got no time to listen to that horseshit
you go get in your car and go on home and find you another book
to read and you tell him next time call me I'll make it right with god
and him both you tell him a sow hog has thirty pigs I'll trade him
my pickup straight acrost sight unseen but I don't want to hear it
now I got work to do who wrote that damn book he must of lived in
New York City his whole life in a whorehouse somewhere just go on
I ain't listening to no more writing like that I don't need it you tell
him if he doesn't know nothing about pigs then don't write about
pigs he should find something else that's all

David Lee

EPILOGUE

What might have been and what has been
Point to one end, which is always present.
    'Burnt Norton'

In my beginning is my end.
In my end is my beginning.
    'East Coker'
                — T. S. Eliot

Months begat seasons begat a year
another
begat a child, another
begat all the successes: advancement,
rank, salary equal to almost one-
half the yearly inflation,
begat respectability, political acumen

voted for all the losers,
Ananias Frogeyes elected, reelected, scholarly insight
studied the use of feminine endings in Milton
by the book, rocked no boats
therefore *was* happy, indeed, passive

Jan made it official,
asked: are you happy?
replied of course. Why not?
asked: are you sure?
replied: I'm very busy. Do you need something?

And on Saturday Jan left
for groceries, I babysat
studied scientific humanism, read essays
she returned, honked
honked, honked

until I came outside, passive
said get this sonbitch unloaded
replied: I beg your pardon
said either get it unloaded
or go back and set on your butt

I'll do it

Saw in the pickup bed
fence wire, twenty cedar posts, sheet iron,
one dozen 2x6 boards, a gunny sack
behold, a gunny sack, *tow sack*
tied with a strand of wire
bailing wore I've seen that before
a voice whispered, where have you been,
Jan? Jan where have you been...
tow sack while I watched
                                  moved

And I *known*
I known whatalls in that towsack's
trouble, break any fence
any man can build or fix
lay in mud, dig holes
belly up to the sun, eat
anything can be eat, gnaw
whatall'll hold still to be gnawed
piss me off worsen anything alive
bring out all the worse
all the best
                in me

behind the spare tire another sack
behold squirmed
tow sack moved, rolled, tow sack
squealed, squirmed, rooted, tow sack
tied with bailing wore grunted

but it caint holt it long
don't worry about being polite
you got to hurry
it'll get out goddam
                        another one.

John B. Lee

SHOUTING WHO WE ARE

After chores
the inconsequential continent
of my father's discarded clothes
dusts the cold shed floor.

Hog-smell perfumed
with the talc of chop
puffed into the sleeves from leaning on the hopper
caught in the fine sift of their hunger
pigs nudge his boots from the trough rungs
and skid through a scarf of straw
circling like someone setting a pocket watch 23 hours wrong
then collapsing where he walks
rubbed from knee to cuff
by their hock-tinged paradigms of dung
and the bristled fabric of their hams
they race
breathe wet-snouted into the stuff he's left behind
their tongues powdered like a unlicked chalk gutter.

One miffed porker crabs the door
so it kicks on its hinges
while 5 cylindered noses
make a pink daisy chain OOOOO
in the chink of light
between the door-bottom and the cement stoop.

Not a lawyer
who hangs his weskit on a chair
loosens his tie, and stagily rolls up his sleeves
to address a jury.
Not a doctor
who wears his stethoscope
like a sacred necklace
touching the cold amulet to your heart.

Not a poet
bangled and rapt
buying the death of each brief moment
with the coins of his eyes
and the coin of his word.
Not a mortician
with the slow sad droop of his hands
draining from each stiff white cuff
like something frozen while it flowed.

But a farmer
up from the barn
unafraid of his nakedness
the shower raining in the little gutters of his flesh
swirls in the drain mouth
milky with what it has meant
to live this day
as we all live with it
shouting who we are.

John B. Lee

PIG DENTISTRY

    1

My father picked up each piglet
tucked him under his arm
like a small watermelon
calmed the squirming
with the certain strategy of his strength.
The razor-sharp trotters
striking out from forelegs
scored his ample belly
with a red welt
like a surgical scar
healed over a missing organ.
My father grabbed these legs
running in air
stilled the surge where futility finally occurred
to the pink little thing
with radiant ears
the light shone through
ears like a bride's nightgown
in the bright bulb
that swayed like a hanged man on its cord
in the sty.

Then he took the wire cutters
from his hip pocket
and opened the pig's mouth
blunting the scream with the size of his hands
and the imperative of his pliers
went snip snip sip
sizing the black teeth
that would needle-prick the sow's teats
like a bad tattoo if they weren't taken
and I see them flying from the mouth
snip snip
like little wire ends they flew, making Gabby Hays

piglets, gummy at the back of their snouts
where they could have ripped your fingertip off
like the corner of a potato chip bag.

Then he sets them down
where after a moment's static revving
of their small hearts
they spin away
spitting out the remnants
of my father's dentistry.

2

What would they have done
in the pre-domestic wilderness?

Made a horrifying shredded rag of her udder?
Pinkened her milk
like berries in breakfast cereal.

We live in such a humane society.
What would those of you who might call him cruel
have him do?
Lend his mind
to the prettifying makers of pork commercials.
Produce quirky little Disney movies
with all that damned big-eyed goodness
as if a boar could not tusk you open
so you spilled like wet groceries
from your own belly skin.

What would you have him do
for the sake of your delusions?
Starve you?

John B. Lee

PRETEND YOU ARE HAPPY

There's a pig riot in the brick barn
and my father goes down
with a cane
down to where those shoats
are taking out their grievances
on one poor weaner
whose side is streaked with toothmarks
his skin already red as a bad essay.
They're brawling
punks who won't quit
driving their jaws in his gut
and circling
while he pants half dead
weaving and stunned where they jam
his ribs like a slammed gate.

My father
goes in there
prying their jaws back
like a hammer clawing tough spikes
but he wins, being human,
and they, being pigs, lose.

What has this pig done?
It is the Lord's day, and everyone is pretending
they are happy —
everyone, that is, except the pigs,
who have made their loud objections,
and children, bored with dull television
and the way the sun moves,
so slow every Sunday afternoon,
like a lazy bachelor looking for salt
in someone else's cupboard.

Jay Leeming

PIG TEACHINGS

As though some angel tired of heaven
had tried to become a stone of the earth itself
and failed, instead stumbling at the doorstep

of granite to awaken in mud as this grunting
wallowing earth-happy beast of squeal
and oink, this screeching dirt-backed dreamer

in the sun and devourer of garbage: and at times
I want to take you for my teacher, O pig,
to learn to live as you do, swallowing

everything, not to refuse the slops the gristle
the rinds or even the paper plates, instead shoveling
it all in as the roaring ancient alchemist in the gut

says yes I accept it all look I am larger look
I am stronger and fatter and glorified and at home
here in the drizzling mud-town that is my heaven now.

Gabrielle LeMay

TURPENTINE

The air smarts. The old man's nose
contracts like a sphincter;
his eyes steam up and go red —
he blames it on his turp-soaked brush.
Pure bristle, it was made
where wild boars roam,
sneering to reveal their dripping tusks,
drool sloozing down
as they rush at you like buses.

This brush works fast.
It slops up/down split/splat
till the empty metal cabinet drops
blam to the floor from the roachy pantry wall
and flips off into shadows.
The old man cries out, his sore, spattered hand
sprained from the shock;
and when the lights blink off
and he's stranded in a pressing, sticky dark,
haunted by the smell of spreading paint —
the grungy hanging fluorescent tube
dead as a cooked snake —
the boars charge.

They never knew love!
They never knew freedom!
Men in suits don't want you to see them
angrily stuffing their own good hairs
into skinny metal jackets
they ram onto ends of flimsy wooden mallets
and strangle into place
shrieking raw hoots of horror — and all
for the palace!?

If I were a boar I'd delight in my own stiff hair!
I'd comb it forward make it stand up tall and wave!
I'd sneer at everyone I saw!
Don't you dare take my hair, you pig!
These are my teeth!
My fangs!
My hooves!
To carve Halloween all over your face!
Slap you silly in a vat of black paint!
Go choke on your own brain-dead
greased-pig race,
you little shit!

James P. Lenfestey

ROADKILL BACON

What a woman, my wife, to think
of picking up a ham and 2 shoulders
from the six hundred pound sow
dead on the side of the road.

Less was left of the car, a Hyundai,
and the driver, a Minnesotan,
the steering column through his heart
like an oven temperature sensor.

Her head was intact and lovely,
her mysterious pig smile
upturned at the corners, as if she
too were experiencing something delicious,

say, pushing through several barbed-wire fences,
raising a hind hoof to the farmer —
sick of his complaints of low prices,
his plaintive soo-eee throughout the long night,

who was gonna kill her anyhow, now
she roots through roadside flower beds
like some gourmet restaurant heard of
but beyond reach, an exotic last meal,

then wheels into the oncoming traffic, determined
to take at least one of them out with her,
pig justice. Not pork, not swine, but pig,
in all her pink glory, lowdown and coming on.

James P. Lenfestey

WHAT THE SMELL OF FRYING BACON MEANS TO ME
— For Blue Spot

I think of her broad, arched
pink back,
smooth high hump of bacon sides
on the trim hoof,
sliding down to her tight
shoulders dotted with a blue
birthmark.
Down further to her
deep-dished, intelligent face,
pink and experienced,
eyes swept with long
white lashes,
ears like pink funnels
swiveling to the sounds
of her passive grunting.

Sliding now over the hump
to her two thick hams
sheltering her billowing spinnaker
vulva
shimmering as she ambles,
rooting for spidery white tendrils
and fat grubs.

Her porcine gorgeousness!
Destined to be an ingredient in
hot dogs!

I smother my grief
in tangy strips
of her taut sides:
Bacon —

salty, warm, glistening,
stretched between
tomatoes,
slathered with mayonnaise.

Those who have tasted
hot dogs
claim for them a texture
mysterious, holy,
yet somehow
utterly familiar.

James P. Lenfestey

WHAT THE SMELL OF FRYING BACON MEANS TO HIM

My God, son, have you ever seen
a cyst-ridden, rutting boar
dragging his toenails over the concrete
pen,
his balls swaying like stone
footballs,
his reluctant snout full
of the insistent scent
of another of his
fifty sows
sloshing into heat?

To him, the smell of frying bacon
means a rest,
a day off,
a few snorts with the boys.

James P. Lenfestey

SOW HAIKU

Try to look a pig
in the eye. You can't. But oh
those long eyelashes!

Nathaniel "Max" Lenfestey

A MAN WHO LOVES HIS BACON

My heart skips a beat before your glistening hams.
Your lean legs catch my eye with their honey glaze.
Your pickled feet call me to taste them,
from the tips of your toes to the salty sweet spaces between.
Something about you is so right it's wrong.

I feel like I am kissing my cousin. But I don't stop.
I eat you with my breakfast, my lunch, my dinner.
Though I know it's a sin I snack on your perfect skin.
And when so much forbidden love leaves me heavy-hearted,
gloved hands reach deep between your sticky ribs
to replace my heart parts with your own.
Thumpity thump. Thumpity thump.

Surely you are my cousin!
So close that my ribs now imprison you.
Your siren sizzle's so alluring I forgot what was right.
I sacrificed my body to you!
I was the burnt offering,
and you repaid me...
with your beating heart.

Thump, pig. Thump!

Denise Levertov

HER JUDGMENT

I love my own humans and their friends,
but let it be said,
that my litters may heed it well,
their race is dangerous.

They mock the race of Swine, and call
'swinish' men they condemn.

Have they not appetites? Do *we*
plan for slaughter to fill our troughs?

The fat ones, despised, waddle large-footed,
their thin ones hoard
inedible discs and scraps
called 'money.' Us they fatten,
us they exchange for this;

and they breed us not that our life
may be whole, pig-life
thriving alongside dog-life, bird-life,
grass-life, all
the lives of earth-creatures,

but that we may be devoured. Yet,
it's not being killed for food
destroys us. Other animals
hunt for one another. But only Humans,

I think, first corrupt their prey
as we are corrupted, stuffed with temptation
until we can't move,

crowded until we turn on each other,
our name and nature abused.

It is their greed
overfattens us.
Dirt we lie in
is never unclean as their minds,
who take our deformed lives
without thought, without
respect for the Spirit Pig.

Denise Levertov

HER VISION

My human love, my She-human,
speaks to me in Piggish. She knows
my thoughts, she sees my emotions
flower and fade, fade and flower
as my destiny unrolls
its carpet, its ice and apples.

Not even she
knows all my dreams.
Under the russet sky
at dusk
I have seen
the Great Boar pass

invisible save to me.

His tusks are
flecked with skyfoam.
His eyes
red stars.

HER PRAYER

Oh Isis my goddess,
my goddess Isis,
forget not thy pig.

Philip Levine

ANIMALS ARE PASSING FROM OUR LIVES

It's wonderful how I jog
on four honed-down ivory toes
my massive buttocks slipping
like oiled parts with each light step.

I'm to market, I can smell
the blade that opens the hole
and the pudgy white fingers

that shake out the intestines
like a hankie. In my dreams
the snouts drool on the marble,
suffering children, suffering flies,

suffering the consumers
who won't meet their steady eyes
for fear they could see. The boy
who drives me along believes

that any moment I'll fall
on my side and drum my toes
like a typewriter or squeal
and shit like a new housewife

discovering television,
or that I'll turn like a beast
cleverly to hook his teeth
with my teeth. No. Not this pig.

Perie Longo

BETWEEN PIGLET AND PUG

It's hard to tell the difference
between piglet and pup
in Minnesota spring mud
if the pup is a pug
both of them streaked in rain
and you're a kid from the city
visiting big sister Nan
helping cut shoats from their moms
so there we all were
covered top to bottom in slop
and circled in squeals
in the business of tagging.
I lifted the runt from the herd
shouting "I've got one," so proud,
brother-in-law Bob turns
and shouts "no, that's the dog!"
and Nan yells "can't you tell
he's not a small hog?" Sure enough
it's barking not squalling
with curled tail wagging
slathers me with kisses
while the piglet skids short
knocks me down
in the pen and we catch it like that
and everything stops
but the story

                and the rain ...

Frederick Manfred

THE FIRST GOOD BITE
— Excerpt from the novel *Green Earth*

Yow! Albert was down and the fat sows were eating him. The sows were fighting over the first good bite of him.

Wild, Free quick looked around. He spotted a wagon rod stuck in the ground near the fence. With both hands he jerked the rod out, then surged up over the plank fence, landed right in the middle of the biting sows, began flailing away at their humped-over dipping necks. At the same time he began kicking at their snouts with his bare feet.

"Albert!" he yelled. "Get up! Get up!"

The old fat sows left off biting Albert and charged Free. Their snouts came yukking straight for him.

Free got mad. What! Pigs dared to tackle him? He was Free Alfredson. A wild shout came out of him. He whaled at their flat snouts with his iron rod so hard and so fast he looked like an eggbeater.

"Get up, Albert! Get out of here, you dumb bastard! While I fight 'em off!"

But Albert just kept laying there in the hog turns and dirty corncobs. His crossed eyes were stuck under his nose.

There was nothing for it but to drop the rod, grab Albert and throw him over the plank fence.

"Yuk ugg! Yukk ugg!" The round snouts of the mad sows came after Free like a bunch of sink drains. One hog got in a good bite just above Free's knee. She ripped open his overalls.

"Yousonsabitchesbitingme!"

In one great leap Free jumped clear over to where Albert lay; grabbed him by the pants and belly; threw him way over the fence. Then, before the sows could wheel around and grab him, Free sprang way up over the top of them, coming up off the ground like a grasshopper, lifting himself sailing over the fence, and landed on his belly beside Albert. Uggh. Both were safe.

The fat sows ruckled up against the plank fence mad at them.

Ma's voice was suddenly crying above Free. "Boy! Oh my boy."

Free rolled over.

There stood Ma in her long green dress. Both her hands were holding up her gold hair.

"Free, Free. What a brave boy you are."

Elizabeth McKim

WHEN THE ELEVATOR STOPPED WE JUST HAD TO LOOK AROUND: PUBLIC HOUSING, INDIANAPOLIS, INDIANA
— *For Etheridge Knight*

When the elevator stopped we just had to look around,
the Black Knight poet and the Poet's woman — see
The pair who wheels the rubber dolls in the baby carriage
The vet who mutters gook gook at three am
The blindman clasping yellow movie ticket stubs
Black Knight Poet and the Poet's Poet woman
Sol who runs the third floor store
Plays cooncan in the lazy afternoon
Chaplain Jack who listens to the triple nickel blues
Lou when he comes out from under beat up cars
undertakes tender care of his ninety year old dad
Hattie Mae who used to run a jook joint on Indiana Avenue
Mr Tongue who drinks with Eth beside the Frosty Tap
Marva Jo who brings us cracklin' bread
Mellow Man and Funky Drum and the Trembler
Buddies from the big top Eth's old school
Tom who likes to hear a woman sing a good catholic tune
The grey haired white dude who calls himself Indian
And copies numbers off the wall out back
Mississippi and Ice Water and Good kid
and the frontbench crones and cronies
and Tony and Tim in wheelchairs
Tough guys once now paralyzed from shoot'em ups
Tim who says I'm permanent when Eth says I'm terminal
And Betty who controls the downstairs desk
And throws out danger signals junkies drunks and loudmouths
We just had to look around
listen to the chorus:
Where is my magic/my meds/my wheels
Where is my check/where are my grandbabies

And Eth says,
Isn't it time to have a pig roast?
Isn't it time to laugh?

Tom Meyer

EATING CHROME

Pigs were a big part of my life as a boy. Each batch of 200 all white pigs lived with us from birth to 6 months old when we shipped them to market and raised another generation. Tending them made me feel capable and grown up. The animate energy of hundreds of pigs compensated for the isolation of farm life. They were young, like me, and had the social instincts and curiosity of adolescent boys on a Friday night. I enjoyed their company. But eventually, watching sow/boar coupling, tending piglet births, feeding them twice daily, shoveling manure, castrating, worming, and then the final prodding of unwilling 200 pound pigs up the ramp to their first and last truck ride lost it's appeal. Unlike the pigs, I was eager to leave the farm. I wanted to live in Minneapolis, go to the University, become an architect.

When I graduated from the School of Architecture in 1972, I got a job with one of my professors. Our work was modern and won awards. I grew a beard and wore wide paisley ties. After a couple of years I bought an old house and a new car, my first, an Opal station wagon. Orange. I thought a German car in 1974 signaled refinement suitable for a young architect. An orange station wagon suggested both sportiness and practicality.

My house had a fireplace that needed firewood. My brother, who ran the family farm now, owned a chainsaw and plenty of deadwood. I drove the Opal to the farm, loaded in the borrowed saw, then drove to the pasture where over the years the rubbing and gnawing of pigs had girdled and killed a dozen trees. As I drove through the pasture gate, the grazing pigs looked up in unison, grass stems in their mouths, two hundred pairs of strangely human eyes fixed on the visitor. Perhaps they thought I was my brother in his truck bringing them corn. I drove near the dead trees, careful to avoid getting mud – or worse – on my new car, parked on a grassy rise and walked to a downed tree. Soon I was lost in the roar of the chain saw. I shut down the saw and turned toward the car, ready to load the satisfying pile of firewood and head back to the city. On the grassy rise was my orange Opal, encircled by pushing and jostling white pigs, like the yolk of great fried egg. Bobbing pigs scratched their backs on my car. Some chewed on the tires. One, his front legs on the bumper, peered into the back window. On the side, two pigs pulled in a tug of war over the chrome trim strip that had once run the length of the car. Pigs were again part of my life.

Charles H. Miller

CONFESSIONS OF A REBEL ROBOT

1

All our anniversaries are departures:
we gobble the bleeding sunrise raw
and swim the burning flood of sunset
to sleep on piles of rumpled maps.

We look at compasses instead of clocks:
direction is our master.
Our staple food is action, and our wildest dreams
speak up at noon. Look — in our language
the largest words are do and go!

Words, words. Bare words. Sharp words:
most functional tools of the human race;
printed words: bare sticks, lined up for meaning,
or hints of meaning. Clues, bird tracks leading
across the sands to the nest of a surviving secret.

Yes, I who pioneer with "do" and "go"
am a poor poet in a rich land!

2

I was born to the northern soil where
lean and somber seasons roared
above a family fed on pancakes, tears.

The crossroads school was a clapboard elephant
that waddled along to flatten corny walls
of a Backland County: the world washed in on me.

Loud births and flabby funerals, dollar-fever,
old-fashioned diseases and new-fangled fears,
the very latest in wars and protested taxes —
all were nothing, were routine nightmares.

My livelihood began in the losing game
of hysterical flats in Depression's fields
beneath Chicago's fanged and fogging mouth.
God and Devil took their turns at me:
choose one of us! O angel of limitations,
the best that I could do was too often myself.

Lean poet with proofs, your place is underground:
"And don't come up until you're a fat success!"

    3
One time beneath a booming year,
when an agent appeared with Everybody's uniform,
I took fit – off to make a killing.
Galloping down a groove with engines at my heels,
running for my life – no, that life.

Dear Robots, with billfold hands, pushbutton brains:
all your who lie seduced by sexless watts beneath
bright blankets – I pant with the payments
on your mortgaged souls!

Once I was one of you.
In the plastic cornucopia of a financed car
I wrestled with bundles of Things and Items:
gadgets ticked beside my heart, my practical heart,
the size of the heart of a pig!

Somehow I got from the trough to stand
in downtown Standardville, and yell:
"This place is strange! Upon my life
am I on the right planet?"
And the wind blew and the chits flew.
My flannelbestos suit fell off
and I stood naked as a human.

    4
Advance! – to new planets of love!
Retreat! – to all that is human!

Stop! — these boiling clouds of outlawed atoms!
Who let them out?
I challenge their right!

I happen to be an overseer of atoms
and I hold inherited shares in our universe!

I sing from the underground of flesh and dream,
pioneering beyond myself
to split the atom that holds the spirit of man.

David E. Moody

THE LAST DAYS OF SUZA'S PET PIG

She gamboled like a rabbit in her youth —
Ambled around to the front yard
To feast on fresh-fallen locquats.

She sniffed out the rice and flax-seed
In the yoga eye-bags like a dog,
And scaled the shelves like a cat to consume them.

But in the end she was pig, all pig, only pig —
Rosie the Great Being.

All that was left in the end was her appetite,
And the great mound of her body.

Rooosie! Rooosie! Suza would call
In a high, sing-song voice.

Rosie would reply with that deep guttural grunt:
Yes, I am here, feed me.

In the end her massive corpulence
Superceded her ability to walk.
She could not even turn upright
Without assistance.

But the mighty river of her appetite
Flowed on unabated.

A night without her bowl
Of warm alfalfa mush
Was intolerable.
She could not rest without it.

And so Rosie's appetite
Finally created a body too great to sustain.

In her last hours, Suza sat by her
And hand-fed her grapes, and watermelon,
And strawberries.
And these last hours lasted three days.

And so we had time to reflect upon Rosie
And her implacable appetite —
That river of continuity
That linked all the days of her life;

All of her days were her last days —
As are all of ours.

It took three men to lower Rosie
Into the dark, delicious earth.

Jim Moore

BLOOD IN OUR HEADLIGHTS,
THE CAR WRECKED, THE BOAR DEAD

     (Italy)

Out of the darkness, men come
     with knives. They work quickly,
muttering back and forth.
     By the time police arrive,
the boar is gone. The foreigners,
     each one of us, stand around
the wrecked car,
     everyone still alive.

     And then

the moment becomes a story,
     cut open as completely as the boar had been,
all of us making use of it
     in whatever ways we need
until our lives and the names
     we were given never to let go of,
go.
     And even laughter and even tears:
gone, along
     with the boar, traceless now
and the unending sound
     of crickets, the brown dust
soaked in blood.

Pablo Neruda

BESTIARY

If I could talk with the birds,
with oysters and little lizards,
with the foxes in dark woods,
with exemplary penguins,
if sheep could understand me,
and lolling woolly dogs,
and carriage horses,
if I could argue with cats,
if hens would listen to me!

It has never crossed my mind to talk
with elegant animals:
I have no interest
in the opinions of wasps
nor those of racehorses:
let them assemble in flight
let them win their racing colors!
I'd rather talk with the flies
bark with the newborn bitch
and speak with the snakes.

When my feet were able to walk
through threefold nights, now gone,
I followed nocturnal dogs,
those starving hobos
that trotted around in silence
rushing toward nowhere
and I followed them many hours:
they didn't trust me
those poor senseless dogs
they lost the opportunity
of reciting their melancholy,
of running with sorrows and tails
through the streets of phantoms.

I was always curious
about the erotic rabbit:
who excites it and whispers
into its genital ear?
That rabbit just goes on conceiving,
ignoring Saint Francis,
deaf to all the nonsense:
that rabbit mounts and mounts again
with his tireless organism.
I want to talk with the rabbit,
I love his mischievous customs.

The spiders waste away
on the simplistic pages
of maddening imbeciles
who watch them through the eyes of the fly
who call them devourer, infidel,
fleshy, lusty, sexual.
To me, this reputation
reflects on the critics themselves:
the spider is an engineer,
a divine watchmaker,
but because of one fly more or less
the idiots can despise her;
I want to talk with the spider
I want her to weave me a star.

I am so interested in fleas
that I let them bite me for hours,
they're perfect, ancient, sanskrit
unstoppable machines.
They don't bite to eat,
they only bite to jump,
they are the leapers of the world,
the delicate, the most intense
and gentle acrobats in the circus:
let them gallop over my skin,
let them spill out their feelings,

let them have some fun with my blood,
only have someone introduce us:
I want to be close with them,
I want to know what I can count on.

I have been unable to form
close friendships with meditators:
of course, I also meditate,
so why don't they understand me?
I'll have to consider this more
while grazing with oxen and cows,
while plotting with the bulls.

Somehow I shall come to know
so many intestinal things
hidden deep within
like clandestine passions.

What does the pig think of the dawn?
They do not sing but hold it up
with their huge rosy bodies
with their hard little hooves.

The pigs hold up the dawn.

The birds eat up the night.

And in the morning, the world
is deserted: spiders sleep,
men, dogs, and wind all sleep:
the pigs grunt, and a day breaks.

I want to talk with the pigs.

Sweet, rough, sonorous frogs,
I always wanted to be a frog one day,
I always loved the pool, the leaves
slender as filaments,

the watercress, a green world
the frogs, lords of the sky.

The serenade of the frog
climbs through my dream and ignites it
climbs like a creeping vine
over my childhood balconies,
over my cousin's nipples,
over the astronomical jasmine
of black Southern nights,
and now that time has passed
let them not ask me for the sky:
to think that I haven't even learned
the hoarse calls of the frogs!

If that's true, then how am I a poet?
What do I know of the geography
magnified in the night?

In this world that runs in silence,
I need more communications,
other languages, other signs,
I want to meet this world.
Everyone has been content
with the sinister presentations
of scrambling capitalists
and systematic women.
I want to talk with so many things
and I won't leave this planet
without knowing what I came here to find,
without forcing the issue,
and people are not enough,
I have to go much farther
and I have to go much closer.

For this, gentlemen, I take my leave
to speak with a horse;
may the poetess excuse me

may the professor grant me pardon,
my week is all booked up,
I have to hear what bubbles.
What was the name of that cat?

— *Translated by Dan Bohnhorst*

Margaret Noori

WORDS OF WIIYAAS

On the occasion of Camp Bacon, hosted by Ari Weinzweig, founder of Zingerman's, author of *Zingerman's Guide to Better Bacon*. Poem in English and Ojibwe.

Red to white / waabshkaa-miskwaa
Raw to ready / jibwaa-ishkwa n'da zaaskookwimi
Carnivores confess / giishpin wi bishigendaaming
As one muscle becomes another / weweni miijinaan wiiyaas
As beads of heat sizzle / n'bwezomi pii gizhaadeg
Oil melting into energy / mide ezhi bimaadziying
So dangerous in excess / aangwaamziin
Still so satisfying / wenesh waayamaan
As midnight sweat / aabita-dibikad minendam
Sweet bacon / wishkobii wiiyaas

Don Olsen

PIGS

I don't trust pigs. They are bewitched
and know how to become other animals.
They have even been known to impersonate
landlords!

Joe Paddock

HENRY AND HILDA

His temper
killed a bull once
with an axe.

And tight: "Henry
pinches his nickel
till the buffalo suffocates."

Hilda would give him
a grocery list to fill at Swanson's.
He'd get there and squint
hard at that list. Couldn't,
just couldn't hand it across
to Swanson. Finally,
slow as the tobacco juice
sliding down his chin,
he'd tear the slip
evenly in half:

"Guess that's
enough groceries
for one day."

Couldn't stand to lose
anything. Saw a small pig fall
into his open well. In an instant
flaring of desire to hold on,
he leapt down after to keep
his pig from drowning. Too late
he realized there was no way
to climb back out.
Water to his waist, Henry held
that squirming pig which, though small,
was still a solid forty pounds and
none too happy to be hugged
down there in the dark.

And now and again it released,
as a pig must, its bowels,
gurgle and slop
into the water. Henry,
within a rising stink,
shifted from foot to foot,
hour by hour, in that icy water,
calling:

"HELP! I'M IN THE WELL!"

But the birds above
simply kept singing.

It meant less than nothing
to Henry that, from down
in his dark shaft in the ground,
stars could be seen in the daylit sky.
He didn't bother himself
with the physics of it.

Why couldn't she hear him?

(Was she, too, treading
at the bottom of a cold well
of decision?)

Hilda finally did
come. Her face hovered
white as the moon above him:

"Henry? Is that you down there
with that pig?"

She lowered the ladder
and Henry struggled stubbornly
up it with the little pig he'd saved
to butcher, but had now
come to know rather well.
Hilda was surprised by the words

that burned from Henry's tongue
as he rose.

"Just take me out back
and shoot me.
No one so foolish as I
deserves to live!"

For the briefest moment then,
as Hilda took the stinking
little armload of hell from him,
Henry saw something warm and forgotten
as stars in daylight
twinkling in her eyes.

Joe Paddock

HOG HUNGER

About ten, clutching
my Red Ryder BB gun, I strayed
into the hog yard
of that farm "Hog" Olson owned.
Why was I there? Did I want
to kill a sparrow
or a pigeon? Town kid,
I hadn't considered
what I'd entered: the winds of the deep
late-afternoon hunger
of fifty hogs, waiting
for the man to come and fill
their jowl-shined trough, deep
with enough slop to ease
the pain of emptiness in them.

A sudden rush of hogs
came at me, hooves and heavy
shoulder bones, as if a downhill
avalanche of boulders.
I faced a circle of burning
little eyes and working jowls, tusks popping
like small caliber pistols. My pants leg
was suddenly ripped, and I retreated
toward the silo, the white barn.
As I backed through the deep,
thick and stinking stuff
that had passed through
the guts of hogs,
old Carl, bald head shining,
was telling me again,
in his Swedish accent, about kids
who'd disappeared forever:
"Holy Yesus, Yoe! Why they couldn't
even find them, you know!"

I'd seen hogs,
in yards like this, take
a dead calf down to glistening bone
in minutes: soft haunch and nose,
long and sloppy uncoiling
ropes of gut, all that sudden
startling pudding, even the brush
at the end of the tail,
and then the bones as well,
the soft calf skull crunched down, contained
by grunt and squeal and the heavy heat
of hog breathing.

It can be said
I'd come to see
my situation
as serious.

Standing before that hog hunger, I knew it
to be the furthest depth of that vacuum
nature abhors, deeper even than the emptiness
in the hole that starts the cyclone
turning. Or perhaps the same. And I,
young gnawer of pork chop bones, knew, too,
for perhaps the first time, that I
was food: butt and belly and brains,
my own, could fill that emptiness
at the center of the storm.

Hogs were raised bigger back then,
and these were three, four hundred pounds.
They stood high on me, above the belt. O,
how solid a thing, a hog, its four hooves
braced in mire. A kid couldn't budge one.
And they'd backed me into a corner
where the round of the silo
met the south wall of the barn.
I was hit by a sudden wave
of inner heat and foreknowledge, felt

the oozing of a sick sweat.
I added a bit to the stink
I stood in, raised
my peashooter BB gun.
Would it help
to take out an eye
or two? Could I
take cold aim
and fire?

Then a sort of grace
of decision hit me:
I'd go at them
screaming and flailing
with the barrel of my BB gun,
as if I were the man
who ran their world. But then
I looked over my left shoulder and discovered
even greater grace: a little ladder
ran up the outside of the silo.

I rose then,
without thought or effort, rose
up the metal rungs, rose above
round little pig eyes that burned
like the tips of torches, saw
sudden bafflement in those eyes
which, the instant before, had had me,
and I laughed, from deep
within me, a laugh
that unfolded out softly
as the wings of that great bird
of old myth, reborn. I hung
on the rungs of that ladder
for maybe an hour, lording it over
those fat, bristling backs.

Then I found my moment

and ran.

Greg Pape

THE HOG BOSS

It must have been a hot day, the air still, sun pushing down
on the big aluminum barn, when the hog boss and his nephew
entered the cloying shade to clean out the pits. One doesn't get
used to the stink. Better to say they were prepared for it,

the way any workers are prepared to reenter the atmosphere
in which they work, once they've worked awhile. The boss
especially. The boss is supposed to know. The fish boss knows
the fish, the road boss knows the road, the fire boss . . . and so on.

But the nephew, when he went down, was not prepared
for the overwhelming fumes, gases of decomposing manure
pooled and etherizing in the pit. The boy began to work,
listening without thought to ruminations of the hogs,

the whole barn an engine, a ticking and liquid rumbling
like a diesel idling, an engine of the afternoon of which
he was a part. He remembered his uncle standing above him
on the metal grates, pacing a little, talking. Then the voice

fading away, body and soul swimming off in different
directions. Later they said the hog boss went down
and hoisted up the boy onto the grates where there
was some air. He must have heard the shovel stop

in the muck and wondered at the long stillness that followed.
He must have called into the pit, and when there was
no answer lowered himself down. He must have been
puzzled at what he found. He lifted the boy out of the pit

as the fumes began to stir his brain and squeeze his heart.
Did he hear hooves on the grates, shit falling like hail
on the crops? Did he call once to the boy, his wife,
his mother? Did he curse the gas or pray to the Lamb?

Did he fall into the engine or fall away from the earth?
Later his wife said, "His thirty-two years of very hard work
were done. We can't put a question mark where the Lord
had put a period." Propped by the door of the barn, shading

his eyes from the sun, the nephew watched as three
men carried his uncle out into the yard, pumped
the chest, and blew their own breaths into his mouth.
He didn't think about it then, as he watched first

one man and then another bow down and place
his lips to the lips of his uncle, how now he
would be the hog boss, and all of his working days
he would remember only part of how it came to pass.

Linda Pastan

GLEANING

Driving from coast
to coast down looped highways,
I notice how the future
we have been speeding towards for years
is receding behind us.
We must have crossed some boundary

and hardly noticed, people
we once hurried to greet
are standing along the roadside
waving goodbye, your grandfather
in his ancestral cap, my mother
holding aloft a flowered hanky.

Still we continue on,
the car radio playing music
we danced to
how many years ago?
When I try to count
I put myself to sleep.

"Talk to me," you say, "don't
doze off." We must watch for
whatever the stubborn flesh
still offers: the smell of hay
sharp and sweet on the air,
desire — that old song.

Look out the car window.
Hogs have been let loose
in the stubbled fields
like heroes in disguise
to find what grains of corn
are left.

SOW

God knows how our neighbor managed to breed
His great sow:
Whatever his shrewd secret, he kept it hid

In the same way
He kept the sow — impounded from public stare,
Prize ribbon and pig show.

But one dusk our questions commended us to a tour
Through his lantern-lit
Maze of barns to the lintel of the sunk sty door

To gape at it:
This was no rose-and-larkspurred china suckling
With a penny slot

For thrift children, nor dolt pig ripe for heckling,
About to be
Glorified for prime flesh and golden crackling

In a parsley halo;
Nor even one of the common barnyard sows,
Mire-smirched, blowzy,

Maunching thistle and knotweed on her snout-cruise —
Bloat tun of milk
On the move, hedged by a litter of feat-foot ninnies

Shrilling her hulk
To halt for a swig at the pink teats. No. This vast
Brobdingnag bulk

Of a sow lounged belly-bedded on that black compost,
Fat-rutted eyes
Dream-filmed. What a vision of ancient hoghood must

Thus wholly engross
The great grandam! – our marvel blazoned a knight,
Helmed, in cuirass,

Unhorsed and shredded in the grove of combat
By a grisly-bristled
Boar, fabulous enough to straddle that sow's heat.

But our farmer whistled,
Then, with a jocular fist thwacked the barrel nape,
And the green-copse-castled

Pig hove, letting legend like dried mud drop,
Slowly, grunt
On grunt, up in the flickering light to shape

A monument
Prodigious in gluttonies as that hog whose want
Made lean Lent

Of kitchen slops and, stomaching no constraint,
Proceeded to swill
The seven troughed seas and every earthquaking continent.

RUSH HOUR FREEWAY SPILL

As cars spill onto the freeway
from downtown office buildings
headed for the affluent suburbs,
a local news helicopter hovers
over a clean-up crew scurrying
to clear pig intestines
from the freeway
like angioplasty clears
clogged cholesterol from arteries.

The local evening news shoves
the slaughterhouse semi's secret
cargo of pig intestines
en route to a Green Bay dogfood factory
in the faces of countless Milwaukeeans
bent over their evening meals.

The woman driving directly behind the semi,
after the mess was hosed off the grill
of her car, said: "This puts me in touch
with my inner vegetarian."

Massive spills of pigshit
polluting North Carolina's rivers
didn't hit home in meat-and-potatoes
Milwaukee the way this did.
And it wasn't a PETA publicity stunt
but a mere traffic accident that forced
the news media to cover meat industry carnage
as dramatically as human freeway fatalities.

Fact:
pig heart valves can replace
failing human heart valves

because pig hearts are most
similar to the human heart.

How many pigs will it take
to supply the overeaters
of 2084? McPig sandwiches
on sale this month.

Vasko Popa

PIG

Only when she felt
The savage knife in her throat
Did the red veil
Explain the game
And she was sorry
She had torn herself
From the mud's embrace
And had hurried so joyfully
From the field that evening
Hurried to the yellow gate

— Translated by Anne Pennington

John Calvin Rezmerski

MISSIONARY WORK

They asked us whether we were Christians. Dick said, "I'm a Lutheran." And they said, "Yes, but are you a Christian?" Dick said, "Lutherans are Christians," and they said, "Well, many Lutherans are." Dick asked, "Which ones aren't?" and they answered, "Well, Lutheranism is a sect, but a Christian is a person-who-accepts-Jesus-Christ-as-his-personal-savior."

"That's me," Dick said. Then one of them said, "Have you been born again?" And Dick said, "Haven't all Christians?" And the other person said, "You can't be a true Christian if you haven't been born again in the spirit." Dick said, "Oh."

They turned to Joe and said, "Are you a Christian?" and Joe said, "I'm a kind of Christian." One of them said, "There's only one kind of Christian, and that's a person-who-accepts-Jesus-Christ-as-his-personal-savior. Are you that kind?"

"That depends," Joe said. "Have you had your pork today?" The other one said, "What does that have to do with it?" and Joe said, "I belong to a pork-chop religion. Lots of other religions can't eat pork chops, but we believe Christians should eat all the chops and spicy back ribs and bacon they want to. We believe God gives us our daily pork, and our duty as true Christians is to accept and partake of pork as a divine treat, sharing it with one another in the name of the Lord. Oh, yes, we believe pork is born again in the smokehouse, and we are born again through eating good ham and red-eye gravy with grits. Just as our Semitic brothers and sisters do the bidding of the living God by feasting on lamb."

"You are making fun of us," one of them said. "No, you are making fun of the Lord," said the other one, "You are making fun of Christians."

"Christians are fun," said Joe. "The Lord is fun, too. For verily, he provideth us with barbecue in the presence of our enemies."

"I've had enough," one of them said. "Let's go," he said to the other.

Joe said, "You're not much fun. Are you Christians?"

George Roberts

PIG

At one time the pig was sacred.
Then he wallowed while Rome burned,
sent troops willy-nilly into terrorist strongholds.

Now, he relies on a pinched vocabulary, grunts
uncomprehending at the rattling teleprompter,
keeps his toilet far from where he eats or lives.

Can learn tricks faster than a dog,
never had no sweat glands, and watches without
comment the sow gobbling up her young.

Pattiann Rogers

BOAR: EVEN THOUGH

He stumps along on his cloven hooves,
his midget legs, bulging, fat, 300 pound
pig, gorgeous, huge porker, jiggling
hams and haunches. He's surfeit,
an abundance of lean muscle and pure
lard, old feast in himself, a perfectly
fulfilled purpose in the flesh.

He stands for all of his swine relatives
and ancient ancestors of 10,000
years — warthog, bush pig, white-lipped
peccary, wooly boar, javelina, bristled
tuskers, acorn shovelers, river
swimmers, acute detectors of thunder
and lightning two days away, keen
rooters of hidden truffles and tubers.

He adores his pignut hickories. He adores
his sows and their wallows.
He can sprint as fast as a squirrel.

Rolling and rooting, settling
into sleep, his great breathing body
inside his grass nest is such a mound
of steady heaving someone might believe
a hillock of forest were quaking to life.

His rumbling, guttural, reverberating
bass snorting, rising from the subterranean
depths of his barrel chest, is the kettle
drumroll of the generous earth
announcing its bounty: *Here he is.*
He eats anything — fungi, grasshoppers,
grains and garbage, eggs, snakes,
mollusks, birds, bark, manure.

*Forgive his stink, forgive his beady,
squinty eyes, his ears like stiff hairy
handkerchiefs hanging over his brow,
his jutting teeth, his dripping digging
snout; for he possesses an intriguing
skull, a brain much superior to a cow
or a dog. And he is senior sire
of countless progeny, his seed so
multiplied "as the stars of the heaven."
He is provision. He nourishes.*

Waddle-trotting away now, see
how his tail in its coil is laughing
at everything he turns his back on.

SELENE'S GENEROSITY

The plains-dwelling warthog (normally diurnal,
rooting for bulbs, tubers, fungi in the noonday
sun) has occasionally been seen feeding
in the light of the full moon.

Coarse black bristles covering her barrel
body from head to shoulders, she is naked
beyond, down to her rump, prissy stick legs,
cloven hoofs. Her weak eyes are tiny
beads buried in the huge, grey gourd
of her head. It would take both arms
of a strong man straining to cradle,
to carry, such a massive head severed.

Even awash in the night perfumes
of worms, molds, grub-rich humus and soil,
she can scent the scat, the spray, menses,
sperm, the spittle of leopard, wolf, feral
dog, approaching boar.

Clair de lune, of course. Lumpy
from her last mud wallow, she grunts
in her odoriferous gut, shovels
through the dirt with her upturned
teeth-tusks, with the cartilaginous
disk of her mucous-dripping snout.
Anyone there to see could see
the pustule-like warts on her misshapen
head shine silver.

By the moonlight, towards dawn, she stretches
on her stomach, dozes in a dew-drizzle.
Moisture gathers in the deep
depression between her petal ears.

One sparrow, two, come to take sips,
a quick splash, at that glittering
pool held tight as pearl in the bristly
cup of her buzzing black skull.

Edith Rylander

OLD MAN STUCKEL TALKS TO THE HOGS

Old beyond milking, his sap all gone to seed,
He moves where he moved as a boy, bringing the cows home.
On dry-stick legs he stumps through the rank sweetness
As he did ninety summers back, eager among the barnyard mysteries.

Here on these acres of his son's farm, in the long gloamings
Of his ninety-sixth summer, he leans on fencing
That creaks like his bones, and talks to the hogs.
Their lively pink noses snoof in the trough.
He tells them how it is. Good harvest, bad harvests,
Blizzards, droughts, corn-growing weather.
Marriages. Wars. A swamp drained.
A field gone back to birches and box elder. The old men in the
          courthouse,
Bearded like God, are slick-faced boys now,
And grandsons of girls he danced with
Stand him to a beer at the Legion Club when he hitch-hikes into town.
All changed, by God. Leaning on dry-stick arms,
He tells them, by God there were women then, not skinny girls.
Real women, farm women, tossing their heads like good mares.
Real dancing, too. Polka, schottische. Moonlight and the smell of sweet
          corn.
Yards of lace. But meat on their bones, by God.

Stroke took his daughter-in-law during the July drought.
She lay nine days, plump hands that knew the warmth under a hen's
          breast
Palms up by her solid thighs.
The German tongue and the laughter all finished. Dying corn
Whispered in the dusty fields like old newspapers.

The day of the funeral it poured. Mourners scurried from car to church.
They brought in gusts of cool air. Scrolled incense, thick as cow's breath
In a frosty barn, shook with the rain-sweet air.

Knocking drops from their hats with scrubbed hands
They muttered, "I hope it don't stop for a week."

After an hour of Latin they took her to the graveyard
To lie under the marble gaze of Jesus eternally dying,
To soften with the rustle of green corn.

After chores and supper, the old man told the hogs.

EMERGENCE

They hold to the secret lands, the brush
slopes, the choked canyons, the twig
tunnels, where the muddied trail
descends into the earth, where the
stream disappears from the sun, where
night takes root at noon. They live
invisibly in the bristling undergrowth far
up canyon or beside Pine Mountain
where storms build bulking blue-black at
dusk striking with lightning and drift
across Chalk Ridge, rubbing through
fire-blackened chaparral, and creep
downslope into the bottomlands at night,
climbing from the black creek bed,
slipping through the dream of alders,
thick-shouldered, heavy-tusked, longsnouted,
the exact tint and weight of
night, huge vague bulking shapes loom
through tule mist, as over some blank and
chosen place they begin to dig, leaving
the tusked earth turned nightside up
before they return to their old holdings,
the secret lands, the brush slopes, the
choked canyons.

Jay Salter

MOONLIGHT

I'm out recording owls from the middle of a quiet meadow,
    listening for compositions balancing the creek's call
in the alders, that delicate fluttering, with the ululation of the owls
    in the firs. And I'm finally locating it, balancing those sounds
in their canvas of quiet, when all hell breaks loose down canyon:
    some disturbance distinctly unowl, some high-pitched feedback loop
with accompanying rumble. Metallic like some slow train wreck. Most unnatural.
    Now it's approaching and I'm wondering what in the world it is,
when into the meadow, into the moonlight, scrambling and squealing,
    screaming and grunting, bursts a whole muddy herd of boars.
Two dozen or maybe more. A galloping chaos of boars,
    a wailing cacophony of boars. A mating herd of boars:
males, all sizes and ages, chasing one rutting sow.
    They mill around the meadow with alarmingly loud collisions
of sound, oblivious to me and all else but their lady.
    For there is no other: she's screeching with prolonged urgency
and annoyance, courted by the dominant boar, who runs his rival off
    into the forest, roaring ferociously as the vanquished squeals
and flees in mortal terror, and the other subdominant boars
    swarm the sow, sniffing, squealing and skirmishing for her favors.
And I'm trying to record this pandemonium, this offered composition
    of pheromones and chaos, but it's too loud, the recorder's overloading,
and I'm taking my headphones off, trying to protect my hearing,
    trying to capture the distant and the near without distortion,
when abruptly all of them gallop off, squealing and careening,
    chasing their muse through the moonlight into deeper portions of the forest.

SUS SCROFA, OR WILD BOAR

Sus scrofa's favorite foods are acorns bulbs and roots. Omnivorous it eats to its advantage everything: fruit eggs newts snakes frogs birds mice. Even kills and consumes the occasional fawn. Most loves gathering mast on the hillside with its brethren under the oak canopy at dusk. Yet can plow a field from dusk to dawn and be home before the farmer comes. Sniffs out corms, or savory bulbs and roots. Works by scent. Snuffles them under the crust of duff, under the fontanelle of earth, resistant in their vaults. Salivates as it works. Works towards the taste. Tusks click and sharpen in the search. Delves and tills for the thing itself. Eschews the abstract. Loves the local. Eats the same things the Indians did: Globe Lily. Mariposa Lily. Two-eyed Violet. Even mouthing the scientific Latin for our beloved common "Blue-eyed Grass" you can root through its *Sisyrinchium bellum* to "Beautiful Pig Snout."

Carl Sandburg

CHICAGO

> Hog Butcher for the World,
> Tool Maker, Stacker of Wheat,
> Player with Railroads and the Nation's Freight Handler;
> Stormy, husky, brawling,
> City of the Big Shoulders:

They tell me you are wicked and I believe them, for I have seen your
    painted women under the gas lamps luring the farm boys.
And they tell me you are crooked and I answer: Yes, it is true I have
    seen the gunman kill and go free to kill again.
And they tell me you are brutal and my reply is: On the faces of
    women and children I have seen the marks of wanton
    hunger.
And having answered so I turn once more to those who sneer at this
    my city, and I give them back the sneer and say to them:
Come and show me another city with lifted head singing so proud
    to be alive and coarse and strong and cunning.
Flinging magnetic curses amid the toil of piling job on job, here is
    a tall bold slugger set vivid against the little soft cities;
Fierce as a dog with tongue lapping for action, cunning as a savage
    pitted against the wilderness,
> Bareheaded,
> Shoveling,
> Wrecking,
> Planning,
> Building, breaking, rebuilding,

Under the smoke, dust all over his mouth, laughing with white teeth,
Under the terrible burden of destiny laughing as a young man laughs,
Laughing even as an ignorant fighter laughs who has never lost a battle,
Bragging and laughing that under his wrist is the pulse, and under his
    ribs the heart of the people,
                            Laughing!
Laughing the stormy, husky, brawling laughter of Youth, half-naked,
    sweating, proud to be Hog Butcher, Tool Maker, Stacker of
    Wheat, Player with Railroads and Freight Handler to the Nation.

THE JUNIOR GOD

The Junior God looked from his place
In the conning towers of heaven,
And he saw the world through the span of space
Like a giant golf-ball driven.
And because he was bored, as some gods are,
With high celestial mirth,
He clutched the reins of a shooting star,
And he steered it down to earth.

The Junior God, 'mid leaf and bud,
Passed on with a weary air,
Till lo! he came to a pool of mud,
And some hogs were rolling there.
Then in he plunged with gleeful cries,
And down he lay supine;
For they had no mud in paradise,
And they likewise had no swine.

The Junior God forgot himself;
He squelched mud through his toes;
With the careless joy of a wanton boy,
His reckless laughter rose.
Till, tired at last, in a brook close by,
He washed off every stain;
Then softly up to the radiant sky
He rose, a god again.

The Junior God now heads the roll
In the list of heaven's peers;
He sits in the House of High Control,
And he regulates the spheres.
Yet does he wonder, do you suppose,
If, even in gods divine,
The best and wisest may not be those
Who have wallowed awhile with the swine?

Anne Sexton

HUTCH

of her arms, this was her sin:
where the wood berries bin
of forest was new and full,
she crept out by its tall
posts, those wooden legs,
and heard the sound of wild pigs
calling and did not wait nor care.
The leaves wept in her hair
as she sank to a pit of needles
and twisted out the ivyless
gate, where the wood berries bin
was full and a pig came in.

Martin Shaw

THE BRINY TUSK
— For the Boar and the Gut

The briny tusk doesn't live on plates!
It curls its legacy around
Its fur-bellied apostle
My gut
That powerjut of defiance
Taunting the mirror
But oddly joyful

The high squeal and lust-salt of its flesh
Belong to the rain soaked God of the Greeks,
Y'know that one, clutching his grapes and leopard,
Born from the thigh of the Thunderbolt.
So the pig is rich in rank, rutting the Olympians,
causing voracious nibbles at English fayres.

And he's low, an erotic rustle through dark grass,
A preacher waving a gun,
A midnightreprieve from a vegan jail,
his flesh stiff leather round our all-too-tender bones.

They tell us to eat it is to play with death,
To jump three steps towards the slippery curb,
A throbbing stumble to indecent joys, snuffling ankles,
and Sundays counting the hard cards of grief.

Wonderful! Where do I sign?

A pig killed an Irish hero
Made sails of his guts
And rode him out into the ebony curls
of an irritable splendour and a foamy repentance.

See? He is tusking my words even now.

So this is no wastrel's flab on me
but a sash of devotion
to the horny, swagger-toothed,
curl-pricked genius of
the fecund woods.

Percy Bysshe Shelley

OEDIPUS TYRANNUS, OR, SWELLFOOT, THE TYRANT
— *From Act 1, Scene 1*

CHORUS OF SWINE

I have heard your Laureate sing
That pity was a royal thing;
Under your mighty ancestors, we pigs
Were blessed as nightingales on mytrle sprigs
Or grasshoppers that live on noonday dew,
And sung, old annals tell, as sweetly too;
But now our sties are fallen in, we catch
The murrain and the mange, the scab and itch;
Sometimes your royal dogs tear down our thatch,
And then we seek the shelter of a ditch;
Hog-wash or grains, or ruta-bagas, none
Has yet been ours since your reign began.

SEMICHORUS

Happier swine were they than we,
Drowned in the Gardarean Sea —.
I wish that pity would drive out the devils
Which in your royal bosom hold the revels,
And sink us in the waves of your compassion!
Alas! The Pigs are an unhappy nation!
Now if your majesty would have our bristles
To bind your mortar with, and fill our colons
With rich blood, or make brawn out of our gristles,
In policy — ask else your royal solons —
You ought to give us hog-wash and clean straw,
And sties well thatched; besides, it is the law!

Jason Shinder

PIGS

When I was a boy the one bad

creature I heard of were pigs,
pigs who rolled in the slime advocating

laziness, poor eating habits, the unimportance

of cleaning, staying in the deep mud
instead of walking a short distance to wash

in the pond. Lethargic, ragged-eared, pink-rusted,

droopy-tailed, heavy-loaded, dull-eyed pigs.
Pigs, who I learned later,

greet each other snort to snort

and at night snuggle up close to one another
and, for some unexplained reason,

sleep nose to nose; pigs who play with piglets

with immense patience, sniffing and nibbling
on them gently before pushing them aside

for another piglet.

Maybe I was absent the day in school
when the teacher said pig-pens are often small

and dark, pigs nosing at straw to make a nest

for another litter taken away, adopted,
moved to an "animal house," because

I thought pigs lived on farms with rolling hills

and green fields and cool winds
banging slowly against the barn doors.

Charles Darwin wrote: "the sooner the pig is fattened

for the butcher, the better." F.E. Zeuer, the historian, said:
"unlike cattle, pigs cannot be driven

and their meat is prone to spoiling and so

we despise them." And William Yanuat, the author
of the first book on pigs, published in 1847, wrote:

"Pigs have feelings in common with each other

and in their eyes is a question for us, Why are you doing this to me?"
I thought I followed the pig

when my mother said that if I didn't clean my face

I would get pigs-eye,
or that my room was dirty as a pigsty,

or that I squinted in the sun like a pig

with small, black-beady eyes
but now I know I was trying like the pig

to get a better view of the world.

Now I know pigs dream and see colors,
pigs move a bale of straw with their noses

so they can stand on the hay

and look out over the gate;
pigs have an ultra-sensitive upward-whining

which seems to curve off the edge of their snouts

when in desire or distress
to signal the other pigs to rush over — oink, oink, oink, oink —

which I once thought was a dirty and dumb sound.

Robert Siegel

THE WHITE SOW OF MARENGO

This little pig stayed home.

Cloud of flesh
you pin the field down
so it won't rise up, rip out the seam of trees
and flap over the swamps to Chicago.

You turn the light to milk
and happily lie
dozing toward China, lending the earth
the gross momentum of your bulk.

As I pass, an incurious eye
follows my head over the fence,
and five chins smile at one
who

unlike you and the sun
drags a flickering shadow over the earth.

Patricia Smith

WHAT KEEPS PLAYING ON THE B-SIDE

Littleton, Ill., April 22, 2009 — During a hog confinement fire in Schuyler County, an estimated 9,000 piglets were killed.

The blazing sputtered, scrambling for a name,
a burnished throat, a language sweet, entire.
Entangled piglets, sweating, tried to claim
space for themselves inside the surging flame,
their squirming hindsides singed by glowing wire

of fence and tool. They struggled for a way
to climb, their squeals a meld of blood and char,
a slow exploding rhumba. Their razored bray
was what a bluesman's shattered heart would say.
The snapping copper ribbons slapped a scar

across the air, and turned their gasping black,
but still they slithered, slippery filthy skins
a squirming blanket weaving, piggyback
and piggy leg and piggy snout and crack
to back, those steely coils of tail, the shins

fusing to shins, while music welled up raw
with lyric meant to complement their dance
of claw and wheeze, a B-side dirge to gnaw
the fence aloose, to God the air. Hurrah
for heat that dons the gaudy garb of chance.

But when the screeching song went dim, the pen
was soup and ruin, the stench of crisping hide
was gospel in the belly. Now and then
a kindled heart would hiss, then hiss again,
the only sign at all that they had cried.

Thomas R. Smith

PIGSKIN

In winter I put on my old pigskin jacket,
its thick, heavy bulk adding five pounds to my weight.
Though the nylon lining is shredded as pulled pork,
the outside's impervious to slings of weather.

My arms and shoulders welcome the fit, wearing
the pig's death as intimately as we wear our own.
The tough leather carries the stubborn will to live
of the swine whose bones bore it before mine.

Where the brown tanning dye has rubbed away,
a more natural pallor emerges, as if to
assert against human fashion the original
pink, never out of style for sow and boar.

Thus attired, I launch forth on the snowy wind,
hard, coarse-grained, aerodynamic as a football
and, like Kinnell's bear-tracking Eskimo hunter,
surviving the storm inside the skin of another.

Gary Snyder

SUS

Two pigs in a pickup sailing down the freeway
stomping with the sway,
      gaze back up the roadbed
           on their last windy ride.

Big pink ears up   looking all around,
taut broad shoulders   trim little legs,
bright and lively with their parsnip-colored skin,
wind-washed earth-diggers
      snuffling in the swamps

They're not pork, they are forever *Sus*:
       breeze-braced and standing there,
                 eternal velvet-dusty pigs.

Robert Southey

ODE: TO A PIG WHILE HIS NOSE WAS BEING BORED

Hark! hark! that Pig — that Pig! the hideous note,
    More loud, more dissonant, each moment grows —
Would one not think the knife was in his throat?
    And yet they are only boring through his nose.

Pig! 'tis your master's pleasure — then be still,
    And hold your nose to let the iron through!
Dare you resist your lawful Sovereign's will?
    Rebellious Swine! you know not what you do.

To man o'er beast the power was given;
    Pig, hear the truth, and never murmur more!
Would you rebel against the will of Heaven?
    You impious beast, be still, and let them bore!

The social pig resigns his natural rights
    When first with man he covenants to live;
He barters them for safer style delights,
    For grains and wash, which man alone can give.

Sure is provision on the social plan,
    Secure the comforts that to each belong!
Oh, happy Swine! the impartial sway of man
    Alike protects the weak Pig and the strong.

And you resist! you struggle now because
    Your master has thought fit to bore your nose!
You grunt in flat rebellion to the laws
    Society finds needful to impose!

Go to the forest, Piggy, and deplore
    The miserable lot of savage Swine!
See how young Pigs fly from the great Boar,
    And see how coarse and scantily they dine!

Behold their hourly danger, when who will
        May hunt or snare or seize them for his food!
Oh, happy Pig! whom none presumes to kill
        Till your protecting master thinks it good!

And when, a last, the closing hour of life
        Arrives (for Pigs must die as well as Man),
When in your throat you feel the long sharp knife,
        And the blood trickles to the pudding pan;

And when, at last, the death wound yawning wide,
        Fainter and fainter grows the expiring cry,
Is there no grateful joy, no loyal pride,
        To think that for your master's good you die?

PIG BEAUTY

Pig
dusted pink
your perfect curve
is all we need to know on earth
of beauty

One hundred bouncing round pig bodies
in one hundred Caucasoid pink skins —
abundance of nakedness

O swine
sprawled in sleep
I marvel at your massive flesh
splayed across the grass in mounds
like tubers bulging hugely
from the earth

Barry Spacks

SINGING THE PIG

Ladies and gents, now I'll sing the pig,
for his tail's Chinese, he's a bank but no prig.
At Bartholomew Fair Shakespeare feasted on mighty
porkers, so Falstaff's "a little tidy
Bartholomew boar –
pig" (2, *Henry IV*)
and what's more, even Zeus took suck of a sow
and the pig looms up big in *The Golden Bough*
(frequent sow-sacrifice, sows being fertile) –
oh, legions of devils by way of the foothole
enter your pig, hence the "scorch marks" on forefeet,
and Jane, Duchess Gordon, down Edinburgh High Street
rode pigback in daylight in 1770,
winning a bet. Pigs are praised for their levity,
damned for their farts and wallows. Impure
to the Jews, and a symbol in *Jude the Obscure*
for nature (sex), the pig stands for flesh,
he's the sneezing baby in *Alice* (God bless
you), and dirty, and greedy, and lately a cop,
but he'll root or die, will grind your slop,
which is why, young maidens, the pig must be sung
(*piga*'s Saxon for "maiden," *hog*'s Gaelic for "young"):
in a poke, in a pie, greased or dry, in a pen:
ladies, the pig! The pig, gentlemen!

David Steingass

RIDING THE MOON-PIG

I felt the sledge drive
through my knees. The pig
may have heard Grandfather's prayer
as the drumclap struck
between his eyes. His streaming blood
spilled the map to nowhere
I knew.
        The pig rose
out of a scalding cauldron
the way half-moons hung
above the barn, gleaming
sleek as a ship's nose. The nested cord
fell from its cavern of belly —
a ghostly rope looped
to the sky's trap door. I lugged
the head by its ears,
poking dragon-teeth. "The bride's
prize," Grandmother said.
"Eyes, ears, brain, and lips."
Her shriek and gnarled laugh
danced along my skin and stood
my hair on end.

Guided by bloody charts
dripped as I walk, my dreams draw
the way. I raise the anchor
by sausage rope. *The Moon-Pig*
shivers in wind from the cold
side of the barn. I stare, lost
in my vague gooseflesh. My orders
cannot be read before dawn.

Joseph Stroud

THE VOICE OF GIOTTO DI BONDONE IN
I WANTED TO PAINT PARADISE

This morning on the Via del Cocomero, I was admiring a basket of
oranges, when a pig broke loose from a passing drove, knocked over
the basket, tried to dash between my legs, and knocked *me* over.

Maestro, are you all right? the vendor asked.
Yes, yes, I laughed.
He was surprised by my humor.
Pigs are very smart, I explained. All these years I've been making
thousands of lire with their bristles. I've repaid them nothing,
not even a bowl of swill. So, how can I begrudge a little revenge?

And besides, how could I tell him, it was good to be down on the
ground a moment. It's true I have painted basilicas in Rome. That
some call me a Master. But brother Francis would love this story.
To be brought to earth by a pig. To be down among all the other
miracles, the oranges scattered about me like small suns, to be
astonished once again.

Su Dongpo

ON THE BIRTH OF HIS SON

Families, when a child is born,
want it to be intelligent.
I, through intelligence,
having wrecked my whole life,
only hope the baby will prove
ignorant and stupid.
Then he will crown a tranquil life
by becoming a cabinet minister.

— *Translated by Arthur Whaley*

Su Dongpo

DONGPO PORK

Created while distracted in a lengthy game of Chinese chess by greatest Song Dynasty (960-1269) poet Su Dongpo (AKA Su T'ung Po, Su Shi). The meat should becomes so tender due to lengthy cooking that you can quite easily pry it away in small pieces with chopsticks. As it is made from a slab of pork belly, there is a lot of fat, but the lengthy cooking time (3-1/2 hours) results in fat sans much of its greasiness. Eat as little of the fat as you choose. The accompanying ginger and plainly cooked broccoli also help offset the fat. You will need at least four hours to make dongpo pork during which time it is simmered twice, braised, sautéed and steamed, during which you can write or recite a dozen short poems.

Serves 4
Ingredients
1 kg (2.2 lb) piece pork belly
2 tablespoons vegetable oil
1 tablespoon tea leaves
4 stalks spring onions
7 cm (3") length fresh, young ginger, sliced lengthways into matchstick widths
Optional: 300 g (11 oz) broccoli, cut into small florets

Sauce Ingredients
1 cup water
8 cloves garlic, lightly crushed
5 slices old ginger (or 7 slices young ginger)
1 tablespoon black peppercorns
4 tablespoons soy sauce
2 tablespoons yellow wine (e.g. Shaoxing wine)
1/2 tablespoon sesame oil
2 tablespoons sugar
Thickening: 1 teaspoon corn flour, 1 tablespoon water, stirred well before use

Method

1) Blanch pork in a pot of boiling water. Throw out water.
2) Put pork back in pot and cover with water. Bring to a boil, and simmer for 30 minutes.
3) Heat a wok and add sauce ingredients. Mix well and bring to a boil. Add pork and cook each surface for a few minutes over a medium heat. Remove pork and drain well. Pour remaining sauce into a small saucepan and set aside.
4) Clean and drain wok. Heat vegetable oil to a medium heat. Fry pork on all sides until it is well browned, making sure skin side is a little crispy.
5) Steep tea leaves in hot water for a couple of minutes, remove and set aside. Place pork in pot of water again–topping up water if necessary. Add tea leaves and simmer for 30 minutes.
6) Place scallion stalks on bottom of a steamer. Transfer pork to steamer. Steam for 2 hours, turning pork after 1 hour (because of long steaming time, you may need to replenish steamer water).
7) Add broccoli to steamer for final 5 minutes of cooking time (boil it separately for 3 minutes if there is no room in steamer.
8) Remove pork to a serving dish and arrange broccoli around it. Reheat sauce in saucepan, adding and stirring in thickener. Pour over pork and serve.
9) Garnish with young ginger slivers, which are meant to be eaten.

Note: The leftover simmer water makes a good pork stock.

Joyce Sutphen

WHAT'S TIME TO A PIG?

I suppose (to a pig)
it means "Come little
piggies and eat
your slop,"

or I suppose it means
learning the lesson
about the brick house and
the wolf,

or it could mean bigger
piggies in their
starched white shirts, stirring
up the dirt

or Snowball and Napoleon
down on Animal Farm
learning how to walk
on two feet,

while somewhere little two
feet, frightened in the dark,
are learning to say
"Kill the Pig!"

Bloody time, cruel time —
ah, there's the question:
what's a world full of pigs
to you?

David Wagoner

THE ORCHARD OF THE DREAMING PIGS

As rosy as sunsets over their cloudy hocks, the pigs come flying
Evening by evening to light in the fruit trees,
Their trotters firm on the bent boughs, their wings
All folding down for the dark as they eat and drowse,
Their snouts snuffling a comfortable music.

At dawn, as easily as the light, they lift
Their still-blessed souse and chitlings through the warming air,
Not wedging their way like geese, but straggling
And curling in the sunrise, rising, then soaring downwind
To the bloody sties, their breath turned sweet as apples.

Robert Penn Warren

GO IT GRANNY—GO IT, HOG!

Out there in the dark, what's that horrible chomping?
Oh nothing, just hogs that forage for mast,
And if you call, "Hoo-pig!" they'll squeal and come romping,
For they'll know from your voice you're the boy who slopped them in
       dear, dead days long past.
Any hogs that I slopped are long years dead,
And eaten by somebody and evacuated,
So it's simply absurd, what you said.
You fool, poor fool, all Time is a dream, and we're all one Flesh, at last,
And the hogs know that, and that's why they wait,
Though tonight the old thing is a little bit late,
But they're mannered, these hogs, as they wait for her creaky old tread.
Polite, they will sit in a ring.
Till she finishes work, the poor old thing:
Then old bones get knocked down with a clatter to wake up the dead,
And its simply absurd how loud she can scream with no shred of a
       tongue in her head.

Cary Waterman

AFTER THE PIG BUTCHERING

What does the pig think of the dawn?
They do not sing but they hold it up.
— Pablo Neruda

I go back two days later
for the skin.
It is dismal weather.
The floor of the shed is wet
where blood mingles with the red paint
and the dark soft manure.
It is a watercolor of confusion and pain,
of the loss of a piece of thought.
The feeding pans are in chaos,
tipped like crazy men around the corners.

I have gone back to pick up the skin.
We left the entrails to droop in a compost heap.
I see them sinking like heat into the ground.
I know parts of them are ovaries.
And there are two blue-lipped stomachs
that seem to smile at me.
The skin is on the roof of the shed.

Carrying it I can tell that it weighs
about as much as my five-year-old son.
It is solid like a head against my breasts.
I begin to like carrying it and squeeze it closer,
rub my cheek into it,
and touch the taut nipples.
They are watchtowers
on both sides of the river we cut open.
I am bringing it home.

Now the smell is on me;
grease on my hands.

I bring it all into my house.
It slides around the doors,
under the beds.
It is pungent
and obsessive.

Cary Waterman

PIG POEM

The pig's ears blossom and fold
like lush jungle lilies.
It is their only attractive feature
except for their shell shaped feet
that try to escape each night into the creek.

Each pig roots under the Prickly Ash,
undermines the foundation of the sauna,
and buries all clothes left lying around.
They are the fat of my existence,
a greasy black skillet.

The Dani of New Guinea have lived forever
on pigs and sweet potatoes.
They have never been Christianized.

Jackson Wheeler

HOG KILLING MEMORY
― *For Deacon Purel Miller*

It happened at the new widow's house
in early September, before the frost.
My dark-eyed father was dead,
and his death made necessary
this killing of hogs out of season.

Mr. Miller stood, cap in hand
in the front yard to say how sorry
he was to hear about the husband's death;
and then he went to work.

My first meeting, at age ten, of this dark man
with great broad shoulders; muscles like polished walnut.
So sure he was of dressing hogs; his confidence
writ large in my uncertain world, pulled
me down the path to the hog-lot and bloody work.

After some forty years, the memory holds. . . .

Come resurrection, that rousing from the sleep
that all shall sleep; when the last star of that last
morning fades in the eastern sky; might I ask Lord
only this: there to greet, without fanfare, in overalls,
standing in Your great light rising,
Deacon Miller, Aunt Nora's son.

J. P. White

ON ANY GIVEN DAY

Out for a morning walk, the wind just laying down
a crease on the lake, I meet a neighbor shoveling mud
after the first downpour in months, who tells me
about Tim who drowned in Carson's Bay
on Saturday night after waking on his sailboat to take a leak,
tripping, conking his head, plunging overboard.
No one on the boat, nor on shore, heard the thunk and splash.

An older father, like me, Tim met his son everyday at the bus.
He took him swimming, boating, fishing
and he played ball with him in the park.
He was always the Dad – tough, tender,
nothing held back by looking at a watch.
At the beach I've watched Tim rub his boy's head
with a towel until his son yelped for him to stop.

I know nothing about Tim's habits, his moods, nothing
about his inner life nor how he kept vigil with his life's knots.
All I know is the seven-year-old son will not have his Dad
to meet him at the bus, and all the boy's thinking about everything
will be forever altered by his father's one misstep.
When I walk past Tim's house, I look for the son behind the screen.
My steps say: look, don't look, look, don't look.

Same day, at the State Fair, I watch a first time mother pig called a gilt,
slabbed in a pen, strain to give birth to the fifth in her litter.
Where any animal might seek the quiet of a barn,
some privacy, the light dim and forgiving,
this gilt is hemmed by hundreds of viewers,
many of them children who eyeball her in a mirror
or on an overhead TV screen, the camera lens shifting

between the live, staggering and sucking piglets
and the isolating throb of her uterine muscles.
When she grunts and pushes, I see a faint ripple jump

at the upper end of the horn of her uterus, and I try to picture her fifth
tumbling down the canal to the other end of the horn,
wondering if her piglet tangles in legs or wraps itself in cord,
the crowd and I knotted and looped, fixed and opened.

The first birth cycle, I'm told by a microphoned woman, is the hardest,
but after that, the litters are larger and easier to drop,
the birth canal now stretched, toughened for the litters ahead,
the gilt now a sow, seasoned in the common trials,
her memory a source of strength for the expectant quivering,
and I think no, it's always hard to come into this world,
hard for the mother and child, hard for the father,

everything we do is much harder than we can imagine
no matter our momentary blindness or full awakening,
just as it must be hard to leave, even when it's quick and unforeseen,
even when no one is witness to the aperture, even when
the wind rattles the halyards and tells you the lake is ready
for your sails to fill and for the next day to come on,
even when a voice says, look, don't look, look, don't look.

Walt Whitman

THAT'S NO METAPHOR ON THE STREETS OF BROOKLYN
— From a Whitman Editorial in the *Brooklyn Evening Star*

"Our City is literally overrun with swine, outraging all decency, and foraging upon every species of eatables within their reach.... Hogs, Dogs and Cows should be banished from our streets."

Morgan Grayce Willow

FARROW

You can see she didn't mean
for the little pigs to get out,
the seventeen Hampshires
scattered across the barnyard
while she stands, mittened hand
shading her eyes, in the open door
to the farrowing pens
opposite the milking parlor.
She must be four, maybe five
in this photo, the old truck's shadow,
framing the right edge.
Nothing but gray in the sky
out to the left, though we know
fields spread beneath it
to the furthest horizon,
and beyond.
Even then the barn looked old,
vertical boards in need of paint
where wood meets concrete.
A broken sled leans
against the foundation.
At the window, one square in four
is broken.

She's too young
to understand the difference
between pork and pigs.
These are small enough
for her to squeeze tight,
if she can catch one,
wrap her short arms
around its belly, her smile
wide as its outraged squeal.
She's too young for the barn
to symbolize anything but home

for these curly-tailed, black
little pigs, the white band
around their shoulders
like the knitted scarf
tucked in her coat collar.

When, at noon, the voice
from the radio drones
prices per hundred-weight,
it's mere chatter to her,
though her dad,
who likes his toast buttered out
to the very crust, and her mom,
who dries her hands on an apron
made from last season's Easter dress,
contend with stacks of paper
in the corner: credit slips
from the feed store,
adding machine tape spilling
over tidy handwritten columns
of numbers, letters
from the bank. They dodge
and scramble yet one more year
to keep this land
in the family.

The coat she wears
in the picture is cut down
from one a cousin wore
in high school. The picture
doesn't show the jelly
on the kitchen table
made from grapes,
overgrown and wild,
climbing the grandmother's
windmill. The eggs at breakfast
gathered from hot nests of hens
the mother hates, her hands
scabbed by their meanness.

The bacon on the dad's plate crisped
to near burn, the way he likes it.
His shock when later
he rounds the corner
and sees hard cash,
loose and drifting
across the windswept yard,
squealing in pleasure to be out
under the cold April sun.

Kevin Young

ODE TO PORK

I wouldn't be here
without you. Without you
I'd be umpteen
pounds lighter & a lot
less alive. You stuck
round my ribs even
when I treated you like a dog
dirty, I dare not eat.
I know you're the blues
because loving you
may kill me – but still you
rock me down slow
as hamhocks on the stove.
Anyway you come
fried, cued, burnt
to within one inch
of your life I love. Babe,
I revere your every
nickname – bacon, chitlin,
cracklin, sin.
Some call you murder,
shame's stepsister –
then dress you up
& declare you white
& healthy, but you always
come back, sauced, to me.
Adam himself gave up
a rib to see yours
piled pink beside him.
Your heaven is the only one
worth wanting –
you keep me all night
cursing your four-
letter name, the next
begging for you again.

Kevin Young

ODE TO CHITLINS
— I. M. *Charlie Barfield 1950-2007*

How do you like them wrankles?
asks my uncle, parish
constable, four
hundred pounds if he's
an ounce & my best
answer may be: *A lot.*

Wrinkled wise man,
you are the kind of kin
I trust few hands
to help with — like his wife my Auntie
Faye's, whose name might
as well be Faith, for that's
what lets me let her

bring you to me
bleached, boiled, run
through the washing machine
till clean, Sweetbread's
sister, tripe's long
lost cousin, you're the uncle
I one day learnt

wasn't really — but I have grown
old enough, & young, to know blood
& family ain't always the same —
so you, I claim. You fed me
when I would have withered
without you, you weather me
like little else. I place

my hands upon you, old
family friend, & pray
you're well the way

my blood uncle phoned
to pray with me after
my father died, when all
I wanted was his best

brisket, smoked slow.
Pork loin's poor brother,
you visit once a year, come
Christmas, if we're lucky — lately
even less. No use
waiting, or complaining —
your guts

are glory. Though your birth
certificate may read *Chitterlings*,
only Holy Ghosts' baptism record
gets your name right, like it did
my daddy's. Despite what
the newspapers say, your name
is not short

for anything, needs
no apostrophe. Those tight jeans
you wear, the ones with creases
ironed in — your linen
suit in winter — are out
of style & you don't care
who knows it. The road may seem long at first

you whisper, but see how brief
it's grown? The trail
may be full of shit
but you can make music
of even that. The last
place you'd look, you're hog
heaven — hard

to get to, much less
clean, you're where

we all end up. You are the finale
of most everything, grow
better with time
& Pace picante. Priest

of the pig, monk
of all meat, you warn me
with your vows
of poverty
that cleanliness is next
to impossible, that inside
anything can sing.

Timothy Young

A BLACK PIG'S HEAD

Down the snowy, Deep Creek Road,
I walk at ease, past the limestone
outcroppings, the nettling white pines,
and a hedge of cast-off wire spools.

Then... in the ditch...
crows on a dead, black pig's head
pick at the eyes and cheeks,
the lips, the tongue and neck bone.

Tracks in the snow show a coyote
sniffed the fat and bristle and left.
Vultures will come, as will the sun
and hawks, and dogs and mold.

When the weather turns there will be worms,
but for now, ice delays the rotting.
Somewhere nearby, in town
or at a farmhouse, pork is in the freezer.

It's always this way, I know...
the living kill to live, or eat the dead,
and these deeds go on and on
like the creek over stones to the sea.

Timothy Young

THE SON OF THE BOAR OF DARTMOOR
— After Ted Hughes's Shakespeare and the Goddess of Complete Being

I am the Son of the Boar of Dartmoor. Gorse and heather are my coat.
I'm Tristan's bane, Adonis's killer, the source of Odysseus' gall.
I'm deep in the shadows of the oldest trees where hunters fear to go.
I'm the obsidian point of the Siberian lance that kills mastodons at the river.
I'm the hump of a bison watching his sons kick up dust in the Badlands.
I'm the first whorl of copal incense lifting from a turtle shell censer.
I'm the last sound of the 1000 year sturgeon leaping off Niagara Falls.
I'm kinetic splendor in the pelican male who swims on Pontchartrain bayous.
I'm the difficult strain in the leather reins holding Tayodeuta's horse.
I'm the footprints that mislead Custer.

I'm a sweet liqueur on a Jazz Queen's lips.
I'm the electrolyte, the honey and pulp in the ice-chilled glass on her lap.
I'm moisture passing through her clothes to her breasts.
I'm the stain on her beaded blouse.
I'm the Popsicle Seller at the Nurses' Convention.
I'm the ship's captain, the bush pilot, the backwoods trapper to whom women writers run.
I steal lilacs, lilies, red apples, and gladiolas just to give you delight. With me, every day is danger and thrills.

My tusk is the sharp moon in the western sky piercing the evening storm.
I'm the constellated boar who tramples the cumulus, eats the sun and shits blood-red horizons.
I'm a crimson sliver shimmering through the green of Aurora Borealis.
I'm a spark from the heart of a star.
I am the Son of the Boar of Dartmoor. Gorse and heather are my coat.

Brad Zellar

PIG TENTS

At night, around the campfires,
just beyond the shadow of the
knife, they tell disconsolate stories
about their fierce history as
mountain savages, fleet fugitives
from conquest, before they were
driven to the flatlands and the
mud and the taunts of
magpies
and men.

Patricia Zontelli

WITH LOVE, *PIGGY*

Behind the peep of my eyes,
I dream of scraps,

slop-tipple, chow. My
bulk-shouldered bounty

trembles with squeal. Hairy,
sweaty, I fall for the corn

you have tossed me, roll
on it until I hurt. Sweetie,

may I show you my scars?

Author Bios and Acknowledgments

Margaret Atwood is a Canadian author, poet, critic, essayist, feminist and social campaigner. She is among the most-honored authors of fiction in recent history. While she may be best known for her work as a novelist, she is also an award winning poet, having published 15 books of poetry to date. From *Selected Poems 1965-1975* by Margaret Atwood, ©1976 by Margaret Atwood, reprinted by permission of Houghton-Mifflin Harcourt Publishing Company, all rights reserved. **Coleman Barks** is a poet and translator in Athens, Georgia. His selected poems, *Winter Sky*, was published last year by the University of Georgia Press. He is also the world-renowned translator of the Sufi mystic poet Rumi. Poems used by permission of the author. **Tree Bernstein** grew up on a sugar beet farm in Washington state where you did not name your pigs. She now lives in Ojai, California, where she has learned to mind her Ps & Qs and a few other letters for her own TreeHouse Press, which you can visit at treepress.com. Poem used by permission of the author. **Wendell Berry** is a poet, novelist and essayist living in Port Royal, Kentucky. Among his most recent books are *The Selected Poems of Wendell Berry*, *Hannah Coulter* (novel) and *The Way of Ignorance* (essays). From *Selected Poems*, Counterpoint 1998, © Wendell Berry, used with permission of the author. **William Blake** (1757-1827) presciently saw pigs as superior beings, given the religious human alternative. The greatest of English book artists, he is the author of many books of illustrated poems, most engraved on copper plates and hand-colored and unappreciated in his lifetime. Daniel Gabriel Rossetti unearthed this poem while rooting around in Blake's notebooks. **Carol Bly** was an influential Minnesota novelist, essayist, and teacher. Her posthumous novel *Shelter Half* was published by Holy Cow! Press to wide acclaim. Poem used with the permission of the estate of Carol Bly. **Robert Bly** is the author of many books of poems, translations, and essays. His recent books include *Reaching Out to the World: Prose Poems* and *My Sentence Was a Thousand Years of Joy*, his second collection of American ghazals. Poems used with permission of the author. **Daniel Bohnhorst** is a poet and translator from Minneapolis. He is currently working on a translation of Pablo Neruda's *Heights of Machu Picchu*. This poem and translation are his first published works, used with permission of the author. **Todd Boss** is the author of the award-winning debut poetry collection, *Yellowrocket* (Norton, 2008). Todd's poems have appeared in *The New Yorker*, *Poetry*, *The Best American Poetry*, *New England Review*, and *Virginia Quarterly Review*, which awarded him the Emily Clark Balch Prize in 2009. Used with permission of the author. **Jill Breckenridge**'s third book of poems, *The Gravity of Flesh*, centers on twelve Minnesota State Fair Poems. "Pretty Ricky" is one of those poems. Jill's awards include Loft-McKnight Writers' Awards in both creative prose and poetry, a Bush Foundation Fellowship, and two State Arts Board Grants. Her memoir, *Miss Priss and the Con Man*, will be published in 2011. Poem reprinted with permission of the author. **Michael Dennis Browne** lives in Minneapolis and is the author of several books of poetry, including *Smoke from the*

Fires and *You Won't Remember This*. His new collection of essays is *What the Poem Wants*, Carnegie Mellon Press. Poem used with permission of the author. **Sharon Chmielarz** lives in Minneapolis. She has published several books of poetry, including *The Other Mozart*, about the composer's sister, Nannerl. Her most recent collection is *The Rhubarb King*. Poem used with permission of the author. **Naomi Cohn** has had work appear in *Water~Stone*, *Fourth River*, *Fish Stories*, and *Main Channel Voices*; also as part of St. Paul's sidewalk poetry project. Other recognition includes grants and residencies, including a Minnesota State Arts Board grant. She lives in Minnesota, having drifted north from her native Chicago. Poem used by permission of the author. **Billy Collins** is a former US Poet Laureate and lives in Somers, New York. His many popular collections include *Sailing Alone Around the Room: Selected Poems* and *Ballistics*. Poem from *Ballistics*, by Billy Collins, ©2008 by Billy Collins, used by permission of Random House, Inc. **Melanny Cowley** lives with her family in Ames, Iowa and is a recent graduate of Iowa State University's MFA in Creative Writing and Environment program. She grew up in the Utah desert, and when she isn't smoking up the keyboard with a great story or making something with or for her two children, you can find her in the high desert fishing, or running on the Bonneville Salt Flats during her frequent trips home. Her previous work has appeared in *Scribendi*, and *Brown Paper* and she serves as fiction editor of Iowa State's journal, *Flyway*.
Josephine Dickinson has published two collections of poetry in the U.K., *Scarberry Hill* and *The Voice*. Her first US collection, *Silence Fell*, was published by Houghton Mifflin in 2007, and she toured the US reading with Galway Kinnell. She wrote this poem for this anthology, used by permission of the author. **Russell Edson** is one of the pioneers of the American prose poem. His many books include *The Wounded Breakfast: Ten Poems*, *The Tunnel: Selected Poems*, and most recently *See Jack* from University of Pittsburgh Press. From *The Childhood of an Equestrian*, Harper and Row, ©1973 Russell Edson, used with permission of the author. **Heid E. Erdrich** is a vegetarian granddaughter of butchers. She won the Minnesota Book Award for her poetry collection, *National Monuments*, in 2009. Poem used by permission of the author. **Louise Erdrich** is the owner of Birchbark Books in Minneapolis, and the author of novels and poems. She along with most of her family and extended family do not eat pigs. She wrote this poem for the anthology, used by permission. **Martín Espada**'s books include *The Immigrant Iceboy's Bolero*, featuring photography by his father, *Trumpets from the Islands of Their Eviction*, and *Rebellion Is the Circle of a Lover's Hands*. In 1996, he won the American Book Award for his collection *Imagine the Angels of Bread*. He has also been the recipient of a PEN/Revson Fellowship, the Massachusetts Artist's Fellowship, and Paterson Poetry Prize, among other honors. "Cade Puerco Tiene su Sábado," from *Al Banza: New and Selected Poems*, ©W. W. Norton, ©2003, and "DSS Dream", unpublished, both used by permission of the author. **Jane Gentry**, 2007-2008 Poet Laureate of Kentucky, is the author of *Portrait of the Artist as a White Pig* (Louisiana State University Press, 2007), *A Year in Kentucky: A Garland of Poems* (Press Eight Seventeen, 2005), and *A Garden in Kentucky*

(Louisiana State Press, 1995). Her honors include a Yaddo Fellowship and a Voices and Visions grant from the National Endowment for the Humanities and the American Library Association. She teaches at the University of Kentucky. Poem used by permission of the author. **Jane Graham George** is an American-born poet who recently relocated to New Zealand. She is the author of *Aoteoroa: New Zealand Poems* and *Library Land*, both from Red Dragonfly Press. From *Bedford Poets 2007 Anthology*, used with permission of the author. **Katharine Grant** sings old folk songs *a cappella* in the style of the worldwide oral tradition — love songs, historic ballads and laments, lullabies and work songs, dance and game tunes used to be a daily part of human life in our ancestors' day. She collects songs from all over the world, with an emphasis in Scots Gaelic, Norwegian, American folk songs, and songs of Robert Burns, himself a collector of old melodies. Traditional song used with permission of the collector. **Donald Hall** is the author of many books of prose and poetry. His recent publications include a memoir, *Unpacking the Boxes*, and a massive selected poems, *White Apples and the Taste of Stone*. He lives in New Hampshire and is a former US Poet Laureate. "Eating the Pig" from *White Apples and the Taste of Stone: Selected Poems 1946-2006*, by Donald Hall, ©2006 by Donald Hall, reprinted by permission of Houghton-Mifflin Harcourt Publishing Co., all rights reserved. **Susan Thurston Hammerski** came of age in south-central Minnesota and has known a good number of pigs of the barnyard and other variety. She is a writer of fiction and poetry, with work published in journals, magazines, and anthologies. Her novel *Song of Grendel's Sister* is on submission under the name Susan E. Thurston. She lives in St. Paul with her family. Poem used by permission of the author. **Han-shan**, or **Cold Mountain**, was a T'ang Dynasty (618-907) hermit poet who lived and wrote from a cave in China's Tientai Mountains. This poem is number 72 in *The Collected Songs of Cold Mountain* (Copper Canyon Press, ©2000), translated by Red Pine (Bill Porter), with a delightful scholarly introduction and photographs. Used by permission of the translator. **Margaret Hasse** is author of three books of poetry, including *Milk and Tides*, *In a Sheep's Eye, Darling*, and *Stars Above, Stars Below*. Originally from South Dakota, she now lives in Saint Paul. As a child, she raised a runt pig, as Fern did, for a future that didn't include a butcher, but the pleasure of cool mud and warm slops. Poem used by permission of the author. **John Southall Hatcher** is Professor Emeritus in English literature at the University of South Florida in Tampa where he has taught for thirty-nine years and served as Director of Graduate Studies for four years, specializing in medieval English literature and creative writing. Dr. Hatcher has published twenty-one books, some of which are translations of his works into Spanish, German, French, and Swedish. Poems used by permission of the author. **Robert Hedin** directs the Anderson Center for Interdisciplinary Studies in Red Wing, Minnesota, and edits *Great River Review*. Holy Cow! Press publishes his selected poems, *The Old Liberators*, and he has translated, with Robert Bly, the Norwegian poets Rolf Jacobsen and Olav H. Hauge. Poems from *The Old Liberators*, ©1998, Holy Cow! Press, used with permission of the author. **Tom Hennen** worked for many years for wildlife agencies in Minnesota and South Dakota. His books include *Love for Other Things: New and Selected Poems* and *Crawling Out the Window: Prose Poems*. Poem reprinted from *Happy Birthday, Minneota*, edited by Tom Guttormsson, Bill Holm and John Rezmerski, Westerheim Press, ©1981, used by permission of the author. **William Heyen** is a professor of English and poet in residence at State University New York at Brockport. He has been awarded two fellowships from the National Endowment for the Arts, a John Simon Guggenheim Fellowship, the Eunice Tietjens Memorial Prize from *Poetry* magazine, and the Witter Bynner Prize for Poetry from the American Academy and Institute of Arts and Letters. His books include *Erika: Poems of the Holocaust* and *The Host: Selected Poems 1965-1990*. Poem reprinted from *Pig Notes and Dumb Music: Prose on Poetry*, by William Heyen, BOA Editions, ©1998, used with permission of the author. **Jim Heynen** grew up on a farm in Iowa, a state where pigs outnumber people four to one. His pig poems have always been his way of honoring the majority around him. They also inspired him to write a few volumes of short stories, novels, and creative nonfiction. Reprinted from *A Suitable Church*, by Jim Heynen, Copper Canyon Press, used with permission of the author. **Bill Holm**, the beloved poet and essayist from Minneota, Minnesota, originated the idea for this anthology. He died in 2009. His books are available from Milkweed Editions, including a posthumous selection of poems, *The Chain Letter of the Soul*. "Pig" reprinted from *Happy Birthday, Minneota*, edited by Tom Guttormsson, Bill Holm and John Rezmerski, Westerheim Press, © 1981, used by permission of the author. "Old Sow on the Road" reprinted from *The Dead Get by with Everything*, Milkweed Editions, used with permission of the author. **Ted Hughes**, the British poet, wrote dozens of poems about animals for adults and children. His voluminous *Collected Poems* is in print in the US from Farrar Straus Giroux. Poem reprinted from *What Is The Truth? A Farmyard Fable for the Young* (Harper & Row, © 1984), permission applied for. **Colette Inez** has published nine books of poetry and has won Guggenheim, Rockefeller, two NEA fellowships and two Pushcart Prizes. She is widely anthologized and teaches in Columbia University's Undergraduate Writing Program. Her memoir *The Secret of M. Dulong* was released by the University of Wisconsin Press in 2005. Poem used by permission of the author. **John Janovy, Jr.** is the author of fourteen books, including *Keith County Journal*, *Dunwoody Pond*, and *Pieces of the Plains: Memories and Predictions from the Heart of America*, and has published over ninety scientific papers and chapters. He founded and directed Cedar Point Biological Station in western Nebraska for the University of Nebraska – Lincoln. He holds the Paula and D. B. Varner Distinguished Professorship in Biological Sciences at UNL. Excerpt from *Conversations Between God and Satan*, © 2010 by John Janovy, Jr., used by permission of the author. **Louis Jenkins**' most recent book is *Before You Know It: Prose Poems 1970-2005*, published by Will o' the Wisp Books, 2009. He lives Duluth, MN most of the time. Poem used by permission of the author. **Rodney Jones** is the author of eight books of poetry, most recently *Salvation Blues: 100 Poems, 1985–2005*. His honors include a Guggenheim

Fellowship, the Peter B. Lavan Award from the Academy of American Poets, the Jean Stein Award from the American Academy and Institute of Arts and Letters, a Southeast Booksellers Association Award, a Harper Lee Award, and the 1989 National Book Critics Circle Award. From *Salvation Blues: 100 Poems, 1985–2005*, by Rodney Jones, © 2006 by Rodney Jones, reprinted by permission of Houghton-Mifflin Harcourt Publishing Co., all rights reserved. **Scott King**, poet, translator and publisher of Red Dragonfly Press, lives in Northfield, Minnesota. His poetry collections include *Leftover Ordinary*, *Lida Songs*, and *Where the Water Falls*. He has also translated several volumes of the Greek poet Yannis Ritsos. Poem used by permission of the author. **Susan Deborah King** is the author of four collections of poetry, the most recent *Bog Orchids*, (Island Institute, 2010). She teaches creative writing and leads retreats on creativity and spirituality in Minneapolis and on an island off the coast of Maine. Poem used with permission of the author. **Galway Kinnell**, author of many collections of poems and translations, lives in Sheffield, Vermont. His *Selected Poems* won a Pulitzer Prize in 1983. His most recent collection is *Strong Is Your Hold*. "St. Francis and The Sow," ©1980 by Galway Kinnell, reprinted by permission. "The Sow Piglet's Escapes," ©1985 by Galway Kinnell, reprinted by permission of the author. **William Kloefkorn** was named the Nebraska State Poet by proclamation of the Unicameral in 1982. A retired professor of English at Nebraska Wesleyan University in Lincoln, he is the author of many collections of poetry and other books, including *Alvin Turner as Farmer* (Logan House, 2004), *Sunrise, Dayglow, Sunset, Moon* (Talking River Publications, 2004), and *Walking the Campus* (Lone Willow Press, 2004). Poems used by permission of the author. **Ted Kooser** is a former US Poet Laureate living in Nebraska. His syndicated column, "American Life in Poetry," reaches millions of readers weekly. His most recent collections include *Delights & Shadows* and *Valentines*. Poem from *Grass County*, Windflower Press, 1971, used with permission of the author. **Kathryn Kysar** is the author of two books of poetry, *Dark Lake* (Loonfeather 2002) and *Pretend the World* (Holy Cow! 2011) and the editor of *Riding Shotgun: Women Write About Their Mothers* (Borealis 2008). She has received fellowships from Banfill-Locke Center for the Arts, the Minnesota State Arts Board, National Endowment for the Humanities, and the Anderson Center for Interdisciplinary Studies. She teaches writing and literature at Anoka-Ramsey Community College and serves on the board of directors for the Association of Writers and Writing Programs. She does not eat pigs, nor has she ever seen them fly. Poem used by permission of the author. **Julie Landsman** is a lover of poetry and an occasionally published poet. She has written three memoirs and has edited numerous books on race, culture and education. She had an uncle who was a farmer on the rocky soil of Connecticut and a brother who grows a fantastic garden in North Carolina. She has a great respect for those who work the land and tend to the animals. Poem used by permission of the author. **Kristin Laurel** is a trauma nurse and mother of three living in Waconia, Minnesota. On the job, she crews an EMS helicopter, which is how she came by the experience recorded in 'Rescue'. She is working on her first book of poems and is a participant in the Master Track program in poetry at the Loft Literary Center in Minneapolis. Used by permission of the author. **David Lee**'s first book of poems was *The Porcine Legacy* (1974). He has raised hogs, worked as a laborer in a cotton mill, earned a Ph.D. with a specialty in the poetry of John Milton, and recently retired as the Chairman of the Department of Language and Literature at Southern Utah University. He was named Utah's first Poet Laureate, and has been honored with grants from the National Endowment for the Arts and has also been honored as one of Utah's top twelve writers of all time by the Utah Endowment for the Humanities. Poems from *The Porcine Canticles*, © 1984, Copper Canyon Press, used by permission of the author. **John B. Lee** was born and raised on a farm near the village of Highgate in Southwestern Ontario. His poems have appeared widely in Canada and abroad. In 1989 he was winner of First Place in the Nova Scotia Poetry Awards, and he received First Place in the Roundhouse Poetry Awards for both 1989 and 1990. His books include *The Pig Dance Dreams*, published by Black Moss Press, from which these three poems are reprinted with enthusiastic permission of the author. **Jay Leeming** is the author of *Dynamite on a China Plate*, a book of poems published by The Backwaters Press. His poems have appeared in a variety of magazines, and he is the recipient of a Creative Writing Fellowship from the National Endowment for the Arts. He lives and teaches in Ithaca, New York, where he serves as Poet Laureate of Tompkins County. He wrote this poem for this anthology, used with permission. **Gabrielle Lemay** was punished at age eight for refusing to participate in a sadistic day-camp greased-piglet race. At age 55, three months before 9/11, she received her MFA in poetry at Hunter College. In 2008, she moved from Manhattan to Ventura County, CA, where the oinkings and squealings of Broadway bus brakes are blissfully absent. "Turpentine" first appeared in *Pandora's Barn*, winner of the 2004 Tennessee Chapbook Prize from Middle Tennessee State University, ©2004. Poem used by permission of the author. **James P. Lenfestey** is a poet and journalist based in Minneapolis. A former editorial writer with the Minneapolis StarTribune, he is the author of a book of essays, *The Urban Coyote: Howlings on Family, Community, and the Search for Peace and Quiet*, and several collections of poetry, including *A Cartload of Scrolls: 100 Poems in the Manner of T'ang Dynasty Poet Han-shan*. Poems used by permission of the author. **Nathaniel "Max" Lenfestey** is a poet, songwriter and environmental biologist living in Capitola, California who happens to have the same last name as the editor and therefore might be his son. Poem used by permission of the author. **Denise Levertov** was a British-born poet who spent most of her life in the US. An influential voice for peace and justice, her many poetry collections include *The Sorrow Dance*, *Candles in Babylon*, and *This Great Unknowing: Last Poems*. Poems reprinted from *Candles in Babylon*, ©1982 by Denise Levertov, New Directions Publishing Corporation, New York, used by permission of the publisher. **Philip Levine** taught for many years at the University of California at Fresno. Now in New York City, he is the author of many books of poetry including *Sweet Will* and *What Work Is*. His most recent book is *News of the*

World. "Animals Are Passing from Our Lives," from *Not This Pig*, © 1968 by Philip Levine, reprinted by permission of Wesleyan University Press. **Perie Longo** is a former Poet Laureate of Santa Barbara, California. As a teenager, she made many happy visits to her sister's farm in Iota, Minnesota where she learned to ham it up and grunt as the occasion required. She has published three books of poetry, the most recent *With Nothing Behind but Sky: A Journey through Grief*. A psychotherapist, she facilitates poetry workshops for Hospice and Sanctuary Psychiatric Center of Santa Barbara and teaches at the Santa Barbara Writers conference and Poets-in-the-Schools. Poem used by permission of the author.
Frederick Manfred (1912-1994) chronicled in his many novels, stories and poems the region of southwestern Minnesota he called Siouxland. His novels include *Lord Grizzy*, *Conquering Horse* and the autobiographical *Green Earth*. Prose passage from *Green Earth*, used with permission of Freya Manfred. **Elizabeth Mckim** teaches at Lesley University and has been Poet Laureate of the European Graduate School for Expressive Art Therapy in Switzerland. Her books include *Body India*, *Boat of the Dream*, and most recently *The Red Thread*. Poem used by permission of the author.
Charles C. Miller grow up on a Depression-era farm in Michigan, and later owned the World Eye Bookshop in Greenfield, MA. As an award-winning poetry student at the University of Michigan, he struck up what became a 30 year friendship with W. H. Auden, leading to the memoir *Auden: An American Friendship*. "Confessions of a Rebel Robot" is from Miller's posthumous collection, *Woodcutting in Winter*, edited by Lynn Perry. Poem used with permission of Lynn Perry. **David E. Moody**, Ph.D., is the former Director of Oak Grove School in Ojai, California, where he worked closely with the school's founder, J. Krishnamurti, and with theoretical physicist David Bohm. He is the co-author, with Kathleen Fisher and James Wandersee, of *Mapping Biology Knowledge* (Kluwer, 2000). He is currently Director of the tutorial service Mind Over Math, and a mathematics and science instructor with Laurel Springs School, and is a friend of Suza and her pet pig. Poem used by permission of the author. **Jim Moore** lives in the Twin Cities, where he was a founding member of the Loft Literary Center. He teaches at the Minneapolis College of Art and Design. His most recent book is *Lightning at Dinner* (Milkweed Editions). Poem used with permission of the author. **Tom Meyer** grew up on a farm near New Prague Minnesota, He graduated from the University of Minnesota School of Architecture in 1972 where he has taught for twenty-five years. Since 1981 he has been a principal in the architecture and interior design firm, Meyer, Scherer & Rockcastle, with offices in Minneapolis and Maryland. He lives in Minneapolis with his wife Martha and has three grown sons. This is his first published poem (really a story, but a good one –Ed.) **Pablo Neruda**, the Chilean poet and ambassador, was deeply influenced by Walt Whitman and shared something of Whitman's expansive spirit. Some of his notable translators into English include Robert Bly, Alistair Reid, and Stephen Mitchell. This is a new translation of "Bestario" by Dan Bohnhorst, used by permission. **Margaret Noori / Giiwedinoodin**, is a poet and teacher who believes

Anishinaabemowin (Ojibwe) must be used creatively in the contemporary world if it is to survive into the future. She is currently Director of the Comprehensive Studies Program at the University of Michigan in Ann Arbor and with students and community members is co-creator of Noongo Anishinaabemjig, a website dedicated to the documentation and revitalization of Anishinaabemowin, www.ojibwe.net. "Words of Wiiyaas" was written for the occasion of Camp Bacon, hosted by Ari Weinzweig, founder of Zingerman's and author of *Zingerman's Guide to Better Bacon*. Poem used with permission of the author. **Don Olsen** printed miniature books for his Ox Head Press in a chicken coop in western Minnesota. He documented a lifelong passion for letterpress printing and book design in his posthumous memoir *A Butterfly Lands on the Temple Bell*. His collected poems remain to be published. Poem reprinted from *Happy Birthday, Minneota*, edited by Tom Guttormsson, Bill Holm and John Rezmerski, Westerheim Press, ©1981, used by permission of Mim Olsen. **Joe Paddock** is the author of several books of poetry, including *A Sort of Honey* and *Dark Dreaming, Global Dimming* from Red Dragonfly Press, and a biography of the environmentalist, Ernest Oberholtzer, *Keeper of the Wild* (Minnesota State Historical Press) He lives in Litchfield, Minnesota. Poems used by permission of the author. **Greg Pape** is the author of nine books, including *Border Crossings*, *Black Branches*, *Storm Pattern*, *Sunflower Facing the Sun* (winner of the Edwin Ford Piper Prize), and *American Flamingo* (winner of a Crab Orchard Open Competition Award). He teaches at the University of Montana, and in the brief residency MFA program at Spalding University. He is currently Poet Laureate of Montana. From *American Flamingo*, by Greg Pape, Southern Illinois University Press, ©2005, reprinted with permission of the author. **Linda Pastan** is a former Poet Laureate of Maryland. Her many books include *Carnival Evening: New and Selected Poems 1968-1998* and *Queen of a Rainy Country*, both from W. W. Norton. Poem reprinted from *Carnival Evening: New and Selected Poems, 1968-1998*, by Linda Pastan, ©1998, used by permission of W. W. Norton & Co. Inc. and by permission of the author. **Sylvia Plath**'s poetry is often associated with the Confessional movement. Although only one collection, *Colossus*, was published while she was alive, Plath was a prolific poet, and her husband Ted Hughes published four other volumes of her work posthumously, including *Ariel* and *The Collected Poems*, which was the recipient of the 1982 Pulitzer Prize. She was the first poet to win a posthumous Pulitzer Prize. Poem used by permission of Random House, Inc., all rights reserved. **Jeff Poniewaz** has taught "Literature of Ecological Vision" via UW-Milwaukee since 1989. His 1986 book *Dolphin Leaping in the Milky Way* won a 1987 PEN "Discovery Award." Lawrence Ferlinghetti called his epic "September 11, 2001" "the best poem I've seen on 9/11." His last name is pronounced Poe-nYEAH-vAHsh and is Polish for "because." Poem used by permission of the author. **Vasko Popa** was a Serbian poet of Romanian descent. His *Collected Poems 1943-1976*, a compilation in English translation, was published in 1978 with an introduction by Ted Hughes. He died in Belgrade in 1991. Used by permission of translator Anne Pennington. **John Calvin**

Rezmerski teaches at Gustavus Adolphus College in St. Peter, Minnesota. His *What Do I Know? New and Selected Poems* and *The Frederick Manfred Reader*, which he edited, are both from Holy Cow! Press. His most recent collection, *Breaking the Rules, Beginning with Ghazals* is from Red Dragonfly Press. Reprinted from *There is No Other Way to Speak*, edited by Bill Holm, ©2004, Minnesota Center for the Book Arts, used by permission of the author. **George Roberts** lives and writes in North Minneapolis. His book of prose poems, *Elfriede's Cat, Notes of a High School English Teacher*, was recently published by Scarecrow Press. Poem used by permission of the author. **Pattiann Rogers** is the author of numerous books of poetry, including *Generations* (Penguin, 2004), *Song of the World Becoming: New and Collected Poems, 1981-2001* (2001), *Firekeeper: New and Selected Poems* (1994), which was a finalist for the Lenore Marshall Poetry Prize; and *Eating Milk and Honey* (1997). The mother of two grown sons, Rogers lives with her husband, a geophysicist, in Colorado. Used by permission of the author. **Edith Rylander** has been writing poetry for 66 years. Her life as wife, mother, gardener, stock raiser, woods dweller, and observer of nature is reflected in her many published writings, including *Hive Dancer*, ©2007 from Red Dragonfly Press. Poem used with permission of the publisher. **Jay Salter**, poet, sound recordist, and piper, lives deep among the wild sounds of a coastal forest in central California, and has had many encounters there with wild boar as well as cougar. He is at work on a collection of poems about the boar titled *Year of the Boar*. His website is www.aldersong.com. Poems used by permission of the author. **Carl Sandburg** (1878-1967) put Chicago on the literary map as "Hog Butcher for the World" in his poem "Chicago." He won the Pulitzer Prize for his *Complete Poems* in 1951 and has remained an American classic. **Robert W. Service** (1874-1958) was my father's favorite poet for his "bard of the Yukon" narrative epics published in 1907 in *The Spell of the Yukon and Other Verses*. Who knew that he had made a Blakean turn toward swine affection and away from Piggish humans and gods. **Anne Sexton** wrote her striking autobiographical poems in seven collections before she committed suicide in 1974. She won the Pulitzer Prize in 1967 for *Live or Die*, and her poems continue to take our breath away through her posthumous volumes. We were pleased and amazed to discover this bit of wild pig music in her remarkable first collection, *To Bedlam and Part Way Back* days before this weighty volume went to press. Permission applied for, Ed. **Martin Shaw** is a mythologist, storyteller, artist, and wilderness rites-of-passage guide from Devon, England. His first book, *A Branch from the Lightning Tree: Ecstatic Myth and the Grace in Wildness*, is available from Ragnell Press in the UK and looking for a US publisher. Poem used with permission of the author. **Percey Bysshe Shelley**(1792 – 1822), the most political of the English Romantics, Shelley wrote this anonymous satire to protest George IV's policies toward the poor. His second wife Mary Wollstonecraft Shelley described its genesis: "We were then at the Baths of San Guliano; a friend came to visit us on the day when a fair was held on the square beneath our windows: Shelley read to me his "Ode to Liberty"; and was riotously accompanied by the grunting of a quantity of pigs brought for sale to the fair. He compared it to the "chorus of frogs" in the satiric drama of Aristophanes; and it being an hour of merriment, and one ludicrous association suggesting another, he imagined a political satirical drama on the circumstances of the day, in which the pigs would serve as chorus – and *Swellfoot* was begun." **Jason Shinder** was the founder and director of the YMCA National Writer's Voice, as well as the director of Sundance Institute's Writing Program. He taught in the graduate writing programs at Bennington College and the New School University. He is the author of *Among Women* (Graywolf Press, 2001) ,and *Every Room We Ever Slept In* (1993, a NY Public Library Notable Book). He died in 2008. "Pigs" is reprinted from *Stupid Hope*, © 2009 estate of Jason Shinder. Reprinted with the permission of Graywolf Press, Minneapolis, MN, www.graywollfpress.org. **Robert Siegel** spent much time as a boy observing his uncle's pigs near Marengo, Illinois. His most recent books are *A Pentecost of Finches: New and Selected Poems* and *The Waters Under the Earth*. He lives in Maine. Poem reprinted from *In a Pig's Eye*, ©1980, University Press of Florida, Gainesville, used by permission of the author. **Patricia Smith** is a poet, teacher, performance artist and author of four books of poetry: *Teahouse of the Almighty*, (Coffee House Press, 2006), a 2005 National Poetry Series selection; *Close to Death* (1993); *Big Towns, Big Talk* (1992), which won the Carl Sandburg Literary Award; and *Life According to Motown* (1991). A four-time individual champion on the National Poetry Slam, Smith has also been a featured poet on HBO's Def Poetry Jam and has performed her work around the world. She wrote this poem for this anthology. **Thomas R. Smith** is a poet and teacher living in River Falls, Wisconsin. He is the author of several books of poems, including a new volume, *The Foot of the Rainbow* (Red Dragonfly Press, © 2010). He is a master track teacher at the Loft Literary Center in Minneapolis. He wrote "Pigskin" for this anthology. **Gary Snyder** is poet, essayist, teacher and pioneering ecological thinker. Among his many poetry collections, *Turtle Island* won the Pulitzer Prize. He won the Ruth Lilly Poetry Prize in 2008. "Sus" is reprinted from *Danger on Peaks*, Shoemaker & Hoard, ©2004, used by permission of the author. **Robert Southey** was born in Bristol, England, in 1774. He was a close friend of Samuel Taylor Coleridge and was appointed Poet Laureate in 1813. He wrote several books including *The Book of the Church* (1824), *Sir Thomas More* (1829), *Essays Moral and Political* (1832) and *Lives of British Admirals* (1833). He died in 1843. **Anne Running Sovik** is a former winner of the Lake Superior Regional Writers Competition and a cofounder, with Patrick Herriges and Susan Stumm Moore, of the White Pine quarterly music and poetry gathering in western Wisconsin. She lives with her husband in Northfield, Minnesota, not too far from a pig farm. Poem used by the author's permission. **Barry Spacks** earns his keep as a persistently visiting professor at UC Santa Barbara, after many years of teaching at M.I.T. He's published poems widely in journals paper and pixel, plus stories, two novels, and ten poetry collections, most recent: *Food for the Journey*, © 2008, Cherry Grove. Poem used by permission of the author. **Joseph Stroud** divides his time between Santa Cruz on the California coast and a cabin in the

Sierra Nevada. Recently Copper Canyon brought out his *Of This World: New and Selected Poems*. Poem from Of this World: New and Selected Poems, Copper Canyon Press, ©2009, used by permission of the author. **Su Dongpo** (1037-1101), greatest of the Song Dynasty (960-1279) poets, wrote no pig poems I can unearth, but deserves inclusion here because he wrote one of Bill Holm's favorite poems, "On the Birth of His Son," translated by Arthur Whaley, that describes the piggish behavior of Cabinet Ministers everywhere, Su Dongpo himself a marvelous exception. In addition, consistent with his remarkable skills as poet, calligrapher, artist and public servant who built the Su causeway over West Lake in Hangzhou, he is credited with the creation of Dongpo's pork, a dish of stewed pork belly rendered delicious through the poet's task of distraction, in this case by a game of Chinese chess. Dongpo's pork is now a culinary signature of the Hangzhou region. Recipe courtesy China Cooks, http://www.eatingchina.com/recipes/dongpo-pork.htm. **Joyce Sutphen** grew up on a farm near St. Joseph, Minnesota, and teaches at Gustavus Adolphus College in St. Peter, Minnesota. Her award-winning books include *Coming Back to the Body* and *Renaming the Stars* (both from Holy Cow! Press). Her newest volume, *First Words*, was recently released by Red Dragonfly Press. Poem used by permission of the author. **David Wagoner** is the author of numerous poetry collections, including *Good Morning and Good Night* (University of Illinois Press, 2005); *The House of Song* (2002); *Traveling Light: Collected and New Poems* (1999); *Walt Whitman Bathing* (1996); *Through the Forest: New and Selected Poems* (1987); *First Light* (1983); *Landfall* (1981); and *In Broken Country* (1979). He was the editor of *Poetry Northwest* from 1966 until its last issue in 2002. He lives in Bothell, Washington. Poem used with permission of author, from *Traveling Light: Collected and New Poems*, © 1999, University of Illinois. **Robert Penn Warren** (1905-1989), regarded as one of the best poets of his generation, twice received the Pulitzer Prize for Poetry, and received the 1947 Pulitzer Prize for Fiction for *All the King's Men*. In 1986 he was named the first Poet Laureate, Consultant in Poetry. The frightening "Go it Granny – Go it, Hog!" from *Promises: Poems 1954-1956*. **Cary Waterman** is the author of four books of poems, and has poems included in the anthologies *Poets Against the War*, *To Sing Along the Way: Minnesota Women Poets from Pre-territorial Days to the Present* and *Where One Song Ends, Another Begins: 150 Years of Minnesota Poetry*. In 2009, she received The Common Ground poetry award. She currently teaches creative writing at Augsburg College in Minneapolis. Poem used with permission of the author. **Jackson Wheeler** was born and raised in the Southern Appalachian town of Andrews, N.C. By profession a social worker, he lives and works in Oxnard, CA. He co-edited the journal *Solo* for 10 years. Poem used by permission of the author. **J. P. White** has published four books of poems. His first novel, *Every Boat Turns South*, was published in 2009. Poem used by permission of the author. **Walt Whitman**, remembered as one of America's two greatest 19th century poets, was also, like the editor of this anthology, once a journalist. That coincidence is marked with the bit of Whitmanic pig journalism included here, taken from the *Brooklyn Evening Star*.

The title is the editor's. **Morgan Grayce Willow** grew up on a small family farm in Iowa, where she bottle-fed runt pigs from early spring farrowing litters. Morgan's poetry collections include *Between and Silk*. Red Dragonfly Press published her ghazal series as a letterpress chapbook titled *The Maps Are Words*. "Pigs" appears in her new collection *Barn*, currently seeking a publisher, used with permission of the author. **Kevin Young** is the author of six books of poems, most recently *Dear Darkness* (Alfred A. Knopf). The recipient of a Guggenheim Fellowship, Young is currently the Attic Haygood Professor of English and Creative Writing and curator of the Raymond Danowski Poetry Library at Emory University in Atlanta. Both poems reprinted from *Dear Darkness: Poems by Kevin Young*, © 2008 by Kevin Young, used by permission of Alfred A. Knopf, a division of Random House Inc. **Timothy Young** is the author a several books of poetry, including *Men Don't Dance in America* and *Building in Deeper Water*, and, most recently, *Herds of Bears Surround Us* from Red Dragonfly Press. He has also contributed to numerous musical collaborations, including *Snow Has Fallen* with the singer-songwriter Yata. Poems used by permission of the author. **Brad Zellar** is a former editor at *City Pages* and *The Rake*, as well as a founding owner of Rag & Bone Books. His writing and photographs have appeared in a variety of local and national publications. He is the author of *Suburban World: The Norling Photos*, and was the recipient of a 2010 Minnesota State Arts Board Grant. Poem used by permission of the author. **Patricia Zontelli** teaches at the University of Wisconsin – Stout. Her books of poetry include *Edith Jacobson Begins to Fly* and *Red Cross Dog*, both from New Rivers Press. Poem used by permission of the author.